To Karren
Thanks fo[r] the cover
and one day you'll
be paid.......hopefully
Lots of Love
Fiona
xxx

How to "Mind Your Gap" Between Stress and Success

How to "Mind Your Gap" Between Stress and Success

Book 1
The Three Keeper Habits to Successful, Stress-Free Living

Fiona M Chapman MA

ChapWell Method Ltd

ISBN: 978-1-80541-758-3 - Paperback

ISBN: 978-1-80541-759-0 - eBook

Book cover designed by Karren Burkett @karrenburkettartist

Other books by Fiona M Chapman

The ChapWell Method:
The 7 Keys to Your Success,
Happiness and Wellbeing

CONTENTS

Foreword

"Wisdom lies in the gap between the thoughts."

Deepak Chopra

Does a day go by when we are not challenged by and even drawn towards the proverbial "edge of the envelope"? This very analogy is more than suggestive enough to set our pulse racing. After all, safety lies within the secure interior, we sense protection from the outside by sturdy walls of containment and let's face it, if our daily lives would just "behave", we may feel no need to expose ourselves to the unknown vastness of the "out there".

As an avid sailor, I have come across in my time many similar analogies for that uncomfortable space that lies outside and beyond our so-called comfort zone. Age-old mariners believed in the existence of mysterious areas of sea where, in their terms, they believed "there be dragons out there". Venturing into that space meant risking not only life and limb but more terrifying for them, the chance of losing one's mind to the unknown and being rendered incapable of finding the way home. Their most valuable tool, the compass, was said to become unusable and untrustworthy, as its arms spun frantically and no longer reflected their true position. Such an example strongly aligns with that loss of direction we experience when our inner compass spins and life's stresses seem insurmountable.

Many myths and legends recount heroes and heroines being lost in unknown worlds, being under the spell of sirens or spirits who played with their minds. The common lesson in many of these tales was the human realisation of the struggle, effort and price of survival.

Archetypal images, such as the labyrinth, also speak to that mythical struggle. The labyrinth is a cornerstone of the myth of Theseus and the Minotaur. The labyrinth symbolises the challenges we face in life, and how it takes courage and determination to overcome them. The function of the labyrinth was to contain the Minotaur, a mythical monster that was half man and half bull and was eventually killed by the Athenian hero Theseus. Daedalus, the creator of the labyrinth, designed it so cunningly that he himself could barely escape it after he built it. To this day, in the ruins of Knossos Palace on the Greek island of Crete, we can marvel at the intricate and very ingenious design of this ancient monument. Its original construction designed to confuse and contain, it has now become a tool of meditation and thought. The labyrinth also helps us gain insight into this time period and its incredible tales of physical and mental challenges. With its many winding pathways, Knossos Palace's labyrinth is indeed an unforgettable experience and a reflection of the human psyche. The modern interpretation and use of the labyrinth, as a tool of reflection and meditation, once more points to the power of transformation from difficulty and stress to a peaceful life practice or ritual.

Fast forward to current times, and despite all the quantum leaping we have done in education, communication and technology, and despite the sea of resources lying at our feet, we could be forgiven for thinking that not much has changed. There is still a deep vulnerability within all of us and the consequential chance that we will also find ourselves in unknown seas and labyrinths of our own. Being mentally lost or indeed "being at sea" is still a reality of life, and an experience which both rattles us yet teaches us to survive.

The objective, however, is not to spend our lives watching every step we take, endeavouring to avoid tipping over the edge or losing our way.

The invitation is more to create and lovingly protect the gap that exists between us and that which seeks to draw us into the confusion, self-doubt and sadness of life's inevitable pitfalls. When we love, protect and start "minding the gap", we can stand on the precipice without fear, knowing that we are choosing the right direction for us. Our inner compass is calibrated and trustworthy and we possess the skills for a successful life, however we personally define that.

Within the gap there is space for everything we need to succeed. Therein lies the wisdom for our discernment, the foundation of our self-belief and the capacity to manifest through transformation. It is the place where we grow, where we can experience events before they happen through pre-play and assessment.

The gap could be seen as the stage on which we have the freedom to rehearse the script of our lives, editing and adjusting the role we choose to play as we navigate our lives. As we set out on this journey of "minding your gap", and as we master the art of stress control, the gap widens, increasing our capacity and confidence to live a great life.

From there, all that remains is for us to shine that light of success, so others are inspired to follow suit and in turn begin minding their gap.

In the words of the author, "It's time to take control of your life, transform your mindset, and manifest the success you deserve."

Frances Tolton, MA Jungian
Life Strategy Coach and Author

Acknowledgements

These two books have been rewritten so many times, until I have hopefully managed to get the ideas across to the reader with ease and simplicity. At times I have stopped writing to do some further study and research to maximise the impact of my methods to help you and my clients. The important thing for me is you, the reader, having the information and power to move away from the struggle of stress and the freedom to choose a life that uniquely suits them.

My grateful thanks to all those many people who listened to me and helped me keep going with the books and the never-ending rewrites. Special thanks to friends, the team who had the know-how to bring this book to life: Jane for her patient editorial skills, Karren for her wonderful artistic skills, and Frances for reading through an enormous splurge of writing and getting me pointed in the right direction, at last! I also have to thank my family and my two awesome sons who are my heroes, Stephen and Peter, who have taught me so much.

A big thank you also must go to Daniel Bedford for helping sort out the title.

Finally, I dedicate this book to Mr Philip; still miss you loads and thanks for loving me.

Introduction

"You must be the change you want to see in the world."

Mahatma Ghandi

You can easily make those changes in your world, dumping the stress and choosing success! So why don't you, I wonder? My many years of working with clients have made it clear to me; we just do not know how to live successfully yet we are taught, from a very early age, how to live stressfully.

My books, courses, journals and recordings are here to help you fill that gap in your education. Showing you how to thrive and create the life you want; not through magic, luck or manifestation—"woo-hoo"—but through the power of your mind.

Your Well-Being

There is a growing awareness of the need to be aware of our and other's well-being and to allow mental health issues to be something that is part of our everyday understanding, including our ability to help by listening and supporting. That is something I endorse, but we can do more than just listen. We can listen to ourselves and others and bring in new success habits rather than reinforcing the stress cycle.

Important Message

While I fully support the growing awareness of our mental well-being and health, an important part of the message is missing and that is it is only ourselves who can look after our well-being, and knowing how to do that and doing it needs to be taught and learnt. Just as we are taught and learn how to keep our bodies fit and healthy, we need to know, explore and feel the success of caring for our minds too.

How to Create Your Best Life

This book, I believe, contains **what we all should and could have been taught** even before we learnt to read and write. That is, **how to look after ourselves**, cope in the modern world and, more than that, thrive as we manage the challenges of modern living and at times take time to heal the scars from our past. Why would you choose not to build a successful life, whatever that may look like for you? How you can easily, at whatever point in your life, take back control and create the life you want, when you know how.

Success or Stress—You Choose

This book is for you if you want to create a successful life rather than a stressful life. Even in this modern-day world where stress is frequently seen as some badge of honour and the only response available to us, few people know how to look after our most critical asset, our mind and its endless ability to support our success and well-being.

How Would You Feel If You Knew You Could Cope No Matter What?

Your mind can be your biggest supporter, or destroyer, or ranging somewhere in between. Why would you allow it to roam between these states without guidance or direction? The answer is simple. We have just not been taught how to direct our mind to full-on support and full control so we can confidently live the life we choose for ourselves. The life that uses our unique talents and strengths, bestowed upon us at birth. To enable us to do more than cope but to thrive.

Use the Book or Put It Down and Keep Struggling

Having worked for many years with clients suffering from stress overload, anxiety, depression, low self-belief and all of the fallout and struggle that a life lived through stress frequently presents, I know change is possible. Consistently, my clients are amazed how, by using these simple exercises (I call them the keeper habits) in their daily life they can start to take back control, build their self-belief, let their confidence flow and start building and creating the life they choose.

Good luck! You deserve a good life and all you have to do is live your life through success, not stress.

CHAPTER 1

The Power Trio: Habits for Stress-Free Success

It really is up to you. We all have a choice but when we do not have the knowledge, the know-how, we are left with the ancient habit of stress and anxiety as the only way to live in the modern world. So choose now the knowledge, the three keeper habits, to lead you away from stress and towards success. I just wonder what you will choose now, more stress or success?

Introducing Your Three Keeper Habits to Successful Living

These simple keeper habits lead you to live successfully, not stressfully, free from the damage of stress and anxiety:

- The first keeper habit helps you claim your inner calm, converting your stress and anxiety habit into calm.

- The second keeper habit boosts your self-belief, maintaining your confidence and self-esteem, freeing you to choose success not stress. Both habits continue to free you from past conditioning, challenges and disappointments which will only pull you down if allowed to linger.

- The third keeper habit helps you identify your unique strengths and talents and use them to meet, rather than deny, your wants and needs.

The Control Myth and Reality

We only have control of ourselves, our inner world, and that is enough to make a difference to our world, life and success.

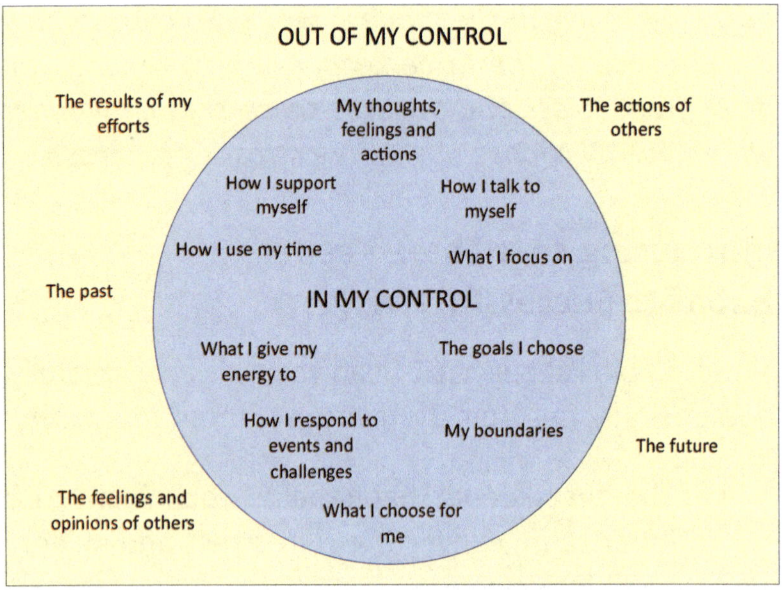

The Three Keeper Habits

Keeper Habit One: Get Back in the Control Area, Lower the Stress

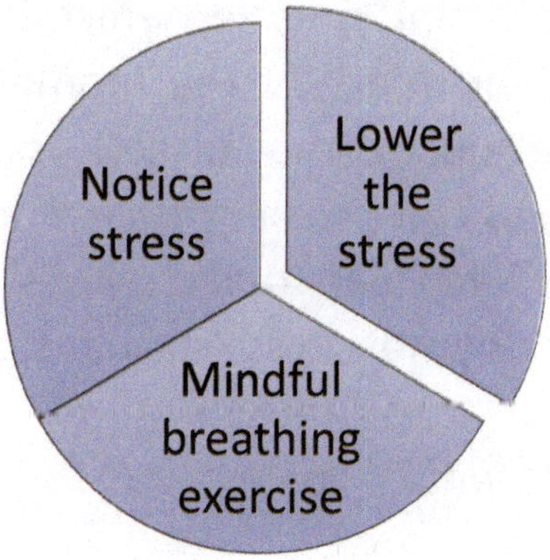

Keeper Habit One is all about reducing the stress you are experiencing, while using that stress as a reminder to bring in the calm rather than the stress.

When you experience:

- stress feelings
- feeling overwhelmed
- worry thoughts
- anxiety
- panic attacks
- fearful thoughts and/or feelings
- struggle to cope

and any other unhelpful stress feelings that make life feel hard for you, just bring in Keeper Habit One.

Using Keeper Habit One

Using the keeper habits is similar to working out our physical bodies, building muscles through practice. Every time you practise Keeper Habit One you are building a new "mind muscle" which brings in peace and calm to your mind. At the moment you have a super strength muscle that directs you to stress; by using that stress muscle as a trigger to build a new "mind muscle" you can quickly build a calm mind muscle. That calm muscle strengthens every time you use it and your stress muscle, through lack of use, gets flabby and weak.

Keeper Habit Two: Keep Self-Belief High

Stress and anxiety are a direct result of damage or gaps in our self-belief. By self-belief I mean our self-esteem and self-confidence combined. If we are feeling capable, able and strong we can deal with anything, anyone and any challenge. We go beyond coping and we thrive. The secret to stress and anxiety is they are only trying to keep us safe, and the more we try to fight them, the stronger they work at keeping us safe by increasing the stress load. The vicious cycle begins, and we start thinking stress is part of who we are, our identity.

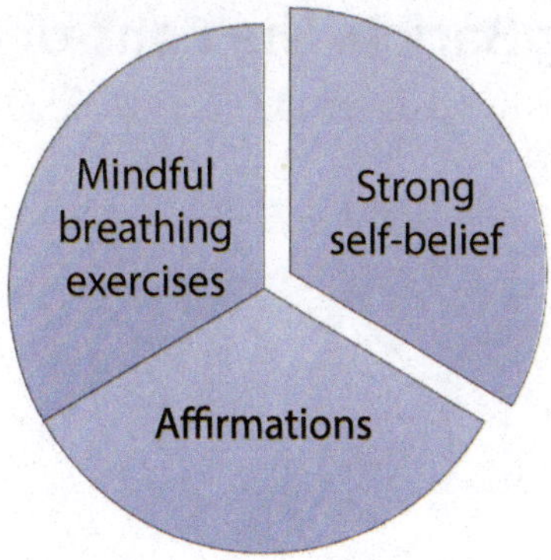

Keeper Habit Three: Go for What You Want and Need

Keeper Habit Three is about getting to know the fearless, confident you, the real you that got buried under all that stress and/or anxiety. Exploring and claiming those unfulfilled desires and wishes that used to be squashed by your fear response, stress. You can now enjoy allowing them to blossom under the real safety mechanism we are all born with: our self-belief, talents and strengths.

You, Working Back in the Control Area

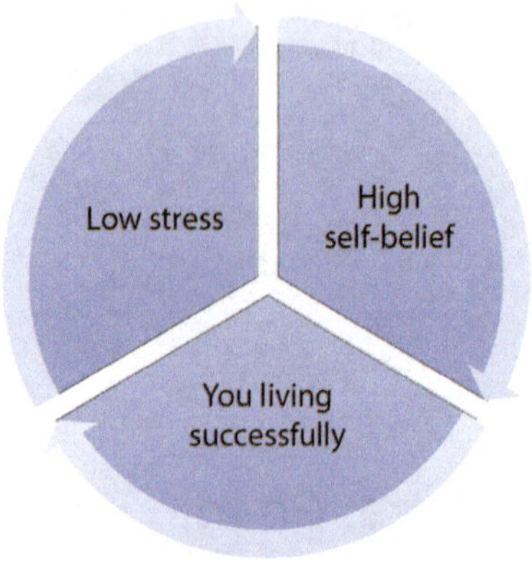

My Mission Is Your Success Free of Stress

When I reached my "retirement birthday", I knew I did not want to stop working while so many people were still trapped in the stress trap of modern living. So many people, once just like me, still did not have the knowledge or choice to live a successful, stress-free life, full of the things they desire, the confidence to know they can and will cope, and experience that inner contentment that brings happiness and successful living.

Past Is Past

Each of us, as we grow, mature and adventure into adulthood have experienced and will experience disappointments, frustrations, losses and gains. We have an unhealthy habit of hanging onto these and storing them in our past memories in a misguided attempt to keep us safe. Unfortunately, this store of past hurts and injustices just brings us down, increases our stress and crumbles our self-belief.

Let It Go

As you use these easy keeper habits you will naturally become more self-aware, more in touch with what is holding you back, driving your stress and therefore more able to let it go rather than generate stress. To help you use your emerging self-, I also include a "remedy store" of exercises so you can now let go of those hurts, disappointments and frustrations when they emerge and return your focus to success and growth.

Believe You Can Make It Happen

Are you ready to change and join the many people before you who have successfully used the three keeper habits to create their unique version of a successful life? You will be changing, and the trick of change is to focus on what you do, never what you do not, do towards the change. Often, we focus on our failure to change and beat ourselves up, which just makes any change so much harder. Focus on what you do towards the change, even just remembering you forgot what to do is a success step, as it means the change is coming into your world. If you forget to do a habit, when you remember, congratulate yourself as you are in the process of a successful change.

Change Is a Process

Part of change is forgetting, giving up and starting again. Try opening every door you come across today with the opposite hand to the one you normally use and notice how you forget, how it feels strange, uncomfortable. Change is about learning a new way to do something and putting it into action. We are humans, not robots, and deciding to change is the first step, not the process of change.

What You Focus On, You Get

The mind, your mind, is a very clever machine and adapts easily and quickly to new instructions, creating new "mind muscles". Using your existing stress habit, or "mind muscle", as a trigger to bring in calm and a peaceful state is the way to permanently stop the stress building. Very often we try to stop feeling stressed by focusing on it and wonder why it just gets stronger, worse. Keeper Habit One helps you focus on what you want and create more peace and calm in your mind.

Interrupt the Stress

"Mind muscles" such as stressors and calm get stronger as you focus on them. Use the unwanted stressful feelings to build the feelings you want. As soon as you notice the stress, use Keeper Habit One and gradually the calm "mind muscle" becomes stronger and the stress "mind muscles" just fade away through lack of use.

Can You Answer Yes to Any of the Following?

- Are you struggling to cope?
- Are you waking up hoping for the best, yet fearing the worst?
- Are you struggling to sleep as your mind worries and plans, and plans and worries some more?
- Are you a hidden super person using all your energy pretending to be okay, to be coping, yet underneath feeling like one more thing will send everything toppling over?
- Do you struggle to switch off and use maybe alcohol, food, binge-watching or something else to distract you from your own feelings?
- Have you given up on your dreams and given in to just coping?

If you can answer yes to any of these or add to the list, you are continually growing your stress mind muscles and adapting them into stress mindsets too. Fortunately, all these mindsets can now become helpful triggers for you to bring in and grow a more relaxed mindset to suit you. Mindsets that will enable you to do not only what you have to do but what you dream about doing too.

The Gap in Our Education

It is not just you; sadly, we are not shown how to work with our magnificent minds. I have spent many, many years working in my therapy practice helping to fill that gap in clients' education, how to do modern-day life and thrive. How to be able to live a successful life according to what we want and need and still feel in control of our life, no matter the challenge, the demands. I have worked with many, many people helping them to understand how we can direct our minds to live in the modern world and not fall prey to all the damage and misery that stress and anxiety does cause us.

The Promise of the Three Keeper Habits

I am not going to kid you and promise eternal happiness if you practise these three keeper habits. I believe happiness is a part of life and real life contains lots of contentment, enjoyment, laughter, struggles, disappointments, frustrations and so on. If you are chasing, or worse still, believing constant happiness is a normal state for us humans then I am afraid you will always be disappointed. Happiness is a state as a result of successful ventures, events and an inner peace and contentment. I suggest to my clients, and to you, focus on growing your inner calm, your self-belief and living your life using your talents and strengths. Focus on feeling good about you and then you will find happiness will flow into your life and all its variations; happiness from contentment, excited happy, comfortable happy and all its other permutations. The three habits free you to live a successful life; a "successful life" is exactly what you want for yourself:

- Able to choose how to live your life
- Feel and know you can cope
- Experience a constant confidence flow
- Manage changes and challenges
- Grow and thrive to get what you want and need

You can control your inner world and be flexible to suit you, not your fears, worries, stresses and anxieties.

Where Are You Now?

Stressed? And maybe you are struggling with change: new job, loss, grief, divorce, becoming a mum, widowhood or any one of those other curveballs life throws our way, wanted or not. Maybe you are just stressed and experiencing stress building into anxiety, low mood and fearful feelings. Frequently, we feel we have little or no control on our circumstances, but they are happening to us and not how we planned. Or maybe you are juggling a demanding job, running your own business, family demands (young and older) and feeling exhausted and running on stress. Determined to keep going but scarily afraid that you will fail or not be up to whatever life challenge you may encounter next.

Or Maybe...

Any struggles are over, the worst is over, yet you find your energy is failing and you feel more and more stressed. Or maybe you think you have always felt like life is a struggle and you are running out of steam, stress is running the show, and your world is getting smaller rather than better as you feel more and more unable to cope.

Do Something Different, No Need to Be Better, Push Harder

I can assure you, it is not you unable to cope, or even the challenge you are going through at this moment, but the gap in your education, that essential lesson most of us never got as we grew up. How do we support ourselves and allow our confidence and self-esteem to hold us steady all the time? How do we use our powerful minds to build us up, keep us strong all the time?

No Magic or Mystery, Just Three Simple Keeper Habits

- Keep the stress low
- Keep self-belief high
- Keep working through your talents and strengths
- Keep clearing any hurdles from the past

The contents of this book are a result of working successfully with many people (myself too) to break out of the stress habit and all its accompanying problems when stress is left to grow. This is the go-it-alone guidebook for clients and for anyone who has had enough of living through stress. Wherever you are in life, with the demands on you right now, it is the perfect time for you to get the habits that will finally break you free, permanently, from the stress trap.

Now or Never

If you find yourself thinking, *Not now, later, I'm too busy to bring the habits in,* I can guarantee that is stress talking, not you, boosted by the gap in your education. Stress will not set you free; you will and can, if only you know how, live through "you" rather than stress and have all those gaps: past hurts, disappointments, letdowns and so on. After all, if you are feeling unwell you adjust your diet to support your physical recovery and it is the same for the mind—you need to adjust your diet to support you and let the confidence flow, able to cope, thrive and succeed, not just survive.

Choose to Win Not Lose Control

The three simple keeper habits help you take back control and change the way you do life. Would you choose to be free of past hurts, disappointments, fears, anxieties and ever-increasing stress? Or maybe you are content to carry on as you are knowing now that stress just gets worse and progresses to anxiety and worse. Your choice, your life.

Case Study: Those That Have Changed Before You

Just yesterday I was in my local chemist and inadvertently jumped the queue. It was confusing, and as I was apologising for my rudeness (I am English, we disapprove of queue jumping) a previous client came up to me. She came across as a very relaxed, confident individual, who looked so different from when I last saw her it took a moment for me to recognise her. She shared with me how so much had changed in her life. Previously she was in a demanding, responsible job with a busy family life, lovely home and good circle of friends (her description not mine) but struggled to cope and stress seemed to be making life just a long struggle. She explained to me she now ran her own successful consultancy, and what was happening with her elderly parents and growing children; as you can imagine, nothing was perfect, there were always things to sort out, but her whole attitude was relaxed, confident in her abilities and relaxed enough to see, enjoying the fun side of life. She looked great and I told her so. Her reply was:

"It's all down to you and everything you taught me. You helped me heal the gaps and choose what I wanted to do, be and feel able to do what I wanted and needed..." (Not exactly what she said but I wanted to use it to explain how damaging the gaps and stress can be when there is a gap in our education.)

Stress Rises as We Feel Our Control Is Threatened

Trying to stop stress or coping by distracting yourself does not work long- or even mid-term, and gets harder to do successfully in the short-term. Stress is designed to keep us safe in emergencies; predominantly, life or death emergencies, so it will push back harder when we try to stop feeling stress or try to ignore it. In fact, as time goes on, we are hardwiring ourselves to experience stress as our first response to anything that may be a potential "threat". Potential threats quickly become anything different, things that are naturally out of our control, ego threats and then our attempts to gain some control just accelerate our stress. Do this a few times and a habit has formed, a "mind muscle" to create stress. Now you know the truth, how to use your mind, you can use these three keeper habits to start forming more helpful habits, which will take over without you having to think about it, bringing calm, confidence, self-belief and real control.

The Gap in Our Education

If we began life learning how to look after ourselves, healing any hurts and disappointments, using them as an opportunity to learn rather than judge, then staying and working in the control area would be simple.

Self-Awareness Grows

Practising and living through success not stress, you will become very quick to notice any barriers, any inner struggles, and the toolkit will show you how you can clear any past barriers and just let them go. This includes recognising you deserve to find out, explore what is bothering you, easily face it and take its misguided power away. Using the mind aid kit to fix that gap and park it in the past, where it belongs, free of any emotional punch to your self-belief, talents and strengths. It is not saying it did not hurt you or punch holes in your self-esteem and confidence; it is about being ready to let go, heal and move on, as the only one feeding the hurt now is you. Letting whatever it is take its correct position in your personal history, the past, over, done with for now and forever.

The Mind Aid Kit

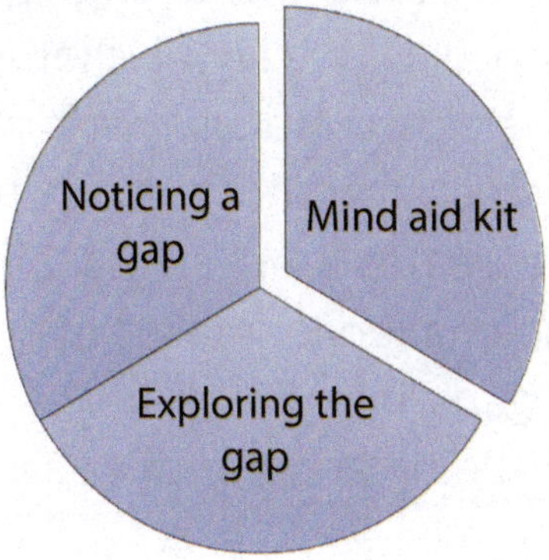

Past Hurts, Disappointments, Negative Experiences and Doubts? Normal

Most, if not all, of us have experienced some hard times, some more than others, some much worse than others, but they all challenge our self-belief and our ability to meet our needs and thrive. It obviously depends on our life experience and our perception of what happened to us; for some it will appear minor or major but each of us will have a range of different coping strategies, most likely all involve high levels of stress. The problem comes when we turn to stress to get us through for too long and too often, then stress actually works in the reverse creating bigger gaps in our self-belief.

This World

Modern life is very demanding, full on and we need all the self-belief we can muster—not more stress, too much stress. The mind can only offer us stress when things are a bit new, challenging, when we are unsure and if stress is quickly discharged it is a good thing, useful, it helps us focus, perform to meet the challenge. However, too much stress never fixes the gap in us. It just creates more stress, blinds our ability to deal with the challenge, makes everything harder, creates bigger gaps in our self-belief and threatens our mental well-being and our physical health.

You Can Use Stress as a Trigger to Heal Any Gaps

As you grow and shape your life you will be travelling into new territory, new challenges, new ways of doing things to suit you, not the old shoulds and coulds. Stress now becomes your friend, a quick jolt to help you focus, do your best, or your indicator that you have a gap in your self-belief. Stress becomes a trigger for you to give yourself what you really need for the challenge you are facing now. The challenge can be big or small, from packing your shopping as quickly as possible in the supermarket queue to presenting your ideas to an audience of thousands. All these things are so much easier once you build and shape your self-belief to match your life, your hopes and desires. Building more self-belief, allowing the confidence to flow, knowing you are enough, just as you are now.

Real Confidence and Self-Esteem = Self-Belief

All Together and Individual Gains from Each Keeper Habit

No matter the stress levels or challenge in your life, until you learn how to derail your stress habit and opt for calm and peace, those challenges and hard times will always be a struggle. Start with Keeper Habit One to clear the stress and enable calm to be your natural state. Everyone knows when we are too stressed, we cease to function according to our ability and can frequently cause more struggles and problems for ourselves. Keeper Habit One is all about using your existing stress habit to trigger your new, chosen habit, Keeper Habit One. This keeper habit immediately connects you with your inner calm, your neutral mind, breaking the stress habit build-up. Each mindfulness-based (Mb) exercise brings a calmer outlook and frame of mind and builds your calm-mind muscle. Research has proven after only two weeks of six minutes a day of Mb exercises your brain changes and your capacity for calm strengthens while the stress response weakens.

Calm or Stress

At the moment, your neural or brain/mind pathway to stress is likely to be strong, even automatic. Each time you do an Mb exercise, you grow a new pathway, and each repeat strengthens the pathway to calm. Unused mind (neural) pathways begin to fade through lack of use and the most used, often repeated pathway becomes the pathway of choice: calm instead of stress. It is the same as our muscle strength: "use it or lose it".

Keeper Habit One as You Go About Your Day

In the next chapter you begin to change your day, your life and let go of the volume and burden of stress interrupting your day, your self-esteem and confidence, peace of mind and happiness. You are free to choose the Mb exercises that suit you best and do them as you go about your usual daytime routine.

Feel the Case from Day One

Keeper Habit One clears the stress and you feel the benefit every time you do a Mb exercise, as well as strengthening your mind's ability to access calm and confidence rather than stress. Imagine a feeling of calm strength rather than stress and more stress, anxiety and all those downer states that take away our power.

This Book Is Your Course and Toolkit for Life

I have put together the three keeper habits, habit by habit, for you to either follow through by yourself or maybe with a group of friends and to continue to support you as you build your life, really connecting with you, and not stress and anxiety. I encourage you to work at your own pace, no competition, just do something each day, just a few minutes and gradually each habit will become a natural part of you. You can also visit www.fionachapman.online for more information on me and the support available.

The Solution for You

Life is busy so I have set out the simple, quick and easy-to-use knowledge in the *Mind Your Gap* books, in online courses, podcasts and recordings so you, too, can choose to live successfully, stress-free for the rest of your life, permanently.

Key Takeaways

The Three Keeper Habits

- Keeper Habit One: Claiming your inner calm and happiness
- Keeper Habit Two: Building self-belief—self-esteem and confidence
- Keeper Habit Three: Living through your strengths and talents

Further Reading

Mindfulness for Dummies
by Shamash Alidina, John Wiley

Visit www.dummies.com and search for "mindfulness" to explore articles and books

A New Earth: Create a Better Life
by Eckhart Tolle

The Structure of Magic
by Richard Bandler and John Grinder

For therapists and a deeper insight into the beginnings of NLP (neuro-linguistic programming)

CHAPTER 2

Mastering the Art of Stress Control

Learn how to tame stress and keep it where it belongs—far from your peace of mind.

Keeper Habit One (KH1): Keep the Stress Low

The first habit reduces your stress by building your capacity to notice stress as it arises and reduce its impact. It builds your calm "mind muscle" while interrupting your stress "mind muscle" from getting a workout, using calm to interrupt those automatic thinking patterns which are constantly triggering more and more stress in you.

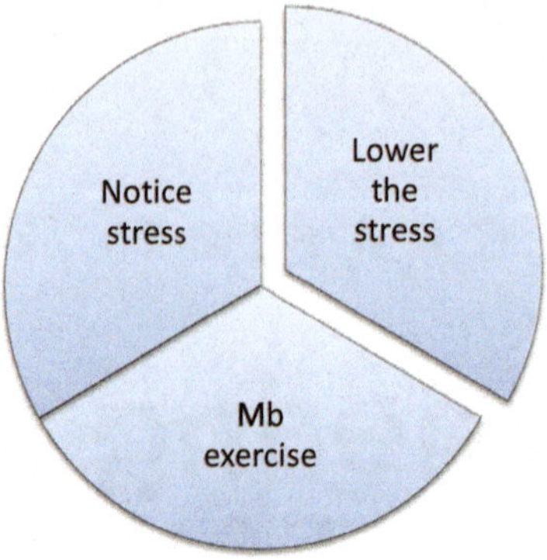

What You Do: Mindfulness-Based (Mb) Exercises

Mb exercises are quick, between one, two and three minutes long, and are based on accessing the power of mindfulness while growing your ability to notice your thoughts, feelings and actions. When you can notice your thoughts and feelings, you can choose and move back into your control area.

Helpful Triggers

Those stress feelings, thoughts and actions now become triggers for you to bring in more helpful feelings starting with calm. Thoughts are just thoughts, not facts, and to select and create thoughts that are going to build you up is now possible and easy. The gap in your knowledge has led you to accept whatever comes into your mind as true for you, a fact, but is it really? The real fact is that thoughts are just thoughts, never facts, unless we choose to make them facts. We always have a choice. Keeper Habit One (KH1) grows your ability to notice and choose to suit you, plus the Mb exercises, which make up Keeper Habit One, give you the space and ability to choose a different state, calm rather than stress, confidence rather than distress.

Our Minds Work Like This

We have a thought which generates feelings/ emotions, which then indicates how we act. Our mind can only give us what it knows; if not guided or directed it will give us something from the past. If our usual response is stress, the habit of stress and all of its thoughts will be our habit in certain situations or times when we are feeling our "safety" is being threatened. By safety, this can mean our identity, how we see ourselves, how we want others to see us, as well as physical and emotional safety.

Nothing to Stop, Just Change Direction

As I have already explained, stopping stress or trying to stop it is our frequent response. Unfortunately, this just triggers more stress as the focus is on the stressful thoughts, feelings and actions. Given our minds work by providing thoughts/feelings and actions around what we focus on, trying to stop stress is still a focus on stress so we just get more stress. By using our stress or uncomfortable feelings as reminders or triggers to focus on calm, it helps us bring in what we want: calm, focus, confidence, etc. The Mb exercises are your calm. Whenever you notice discomfort or stress then use an Mb exercise to bring in a more helpful state, calm and focused on what is really happening now. What is happening now needs your full attention, not what could happen, may happen or happened last time but now, so you can manage the situation to the best of your ability. Much better than getting highjacked by the past, maybes or possibilities, all of course never helpful or supportive or you would not experience stress!

Keeper Habit One Changes How Our Minds React

Research has found the benefits of five to six minutes of daily mindfulness practice (this does not need to be all in one go) will begin to emerge after just two weeks. You do not have to wait two weeks though. Each exercise helps us experience calm, thus shrinking the stress response habit and getting you off the stress, anxiety highway.

You can use these exercises as a stepping stone towards meditation or stick with the exercises to bring in the benefits of mindfulness as you go about your day. To start, use the Mb exercises as you go about your day, every day, at least three times a day. At the end of this chapter there are a range of Mb exercises for you to try and find your personal favourite(s).

Some other things for you to explore and think about as you get Keeper Habit One installed.

Carrots, Not Sticks

Following the exercises and bringing in self-care on a daily basis will be a change and as with all changes you will go through the change process, more about change later. For now, I want you to focus on what you have achieved and congratulate yourself every time you remember to use one of the techniques. I'll also show you how to habit tag to help you on your way. For now, just remember, forgetting and remembering is part of your change journey. It's a normal part of change. When you remember to use these techniques, always congratulate yourself. Forget beating yourself up or, worse still, giving up.

Speaking Carrots, Not Sticks or Bricks!

Just as I am asking you to say kind, supportive things to yourself, it's important to start framing your words in the positive too. That is still speaking your truth but opening up the possibilities rather than closing your mind, options and possibilities down. When you speak not only are others listening but you are too, so make sure it's positive. For example, "I don't like carrots" works better as "I much prefer peas to carrots". Or in my case I could say "I hate tea", which I do and have a really gruesome memory attached to tea and I just remind myself of the link between gruesome and the yucky taste of tea and that's all I'm left with in that moment. However, if I say "I don't like tea. I much prefer coffee", I'm now thinking of a lovely cup of smooth, freshly brewed coffee. Think on it. What feelings or thoughts do you want to bring into your now?

Saying It How It Is—Positively

Making negative judgements closes things down and raises your awareness of what is not okay for you; negative emotions and feelings become your now experience. They were your past maybe and you cannot change that, but you can create a better now. It does not change what is not okay with you but keeps your mood up, feeling capable of dealing with anything that is not okay. Avoidance is not the result you are working towards here, rather letting the past settle into the past and focusing on creating a better now.

Judgement Becomes Discernment and Gives You Options

It's removing the judgement and using discernment, deciding what attracts you or suits you more. Rather than saying "I don't like that" or "I don't agree with that" or "you're wrong", you use it to bring into your mind what you do like, what attracts you or what you agree with and suits you better. For example, if you find yourself saying, or thinking, "I don't agree with that" rather than judge consider instead "what would be more agreeable to me?" For example, if it is something you've seen and find yourself judging as "bad" think of it as "not for me" and "I prefer to see, do or hear..." Maybe someone says something you are not attracted to, even firmly against; it is about acknowledging it as something you are not attracted to and voicing your preferred viewpoint, if it's a conversation you want to get into, or just moving closer towards your preference. Whereas, if you just say or think I don't agree, all you get is the disagreement or disliking thoughts, feelings and actions. When you say out loud or even think about things using discernment you train your mind to respond positively (if not that, what do I like/prefer?) and provide options for growth and really knowing yourself.

You always have a choice about how you engage with yourself, others and your world, to include what suits you and recognise what does not work for you. You are taking the opportunity to explore what you prefer. Judgement alone leaves you stuck, just feeling it is not okay and likely to trigger other negative states that can be equally unhelpful to your peace of mind.

Judgement Has a Place in Our Life Too

Judgement is not wrong and can be very useful in helping us make decisions and learning to grow. However, if judgements grow too much, become too rigid, they close down our world, only allow for good or bad or disinterest, and do not act as springboards for creating our now, our future and all the other things that we enjoy, experience, desire, aspire to and achieve. Judgements quickly lead us to form beliefs through which we view the world, even things we know nothing about.

Beliefs and Judgements

Our beliefs and views of the world then form our rules for living; beliefs develop patterns in our external world and our internal thinking. That's why many people can find themselves in similar relationships or experiencing similar relationship patterns—for example, the bully at work, the unsupportive partner. Frequently we inadvertently create these things in our lives through our beliefs, our rules for living. It's a bit like saying you don't like chairs. How can this be as there are so many different chairs, different colours and sizes, and if you are desperate to sit down after a long time standing on your feet then any chair will feel beneficial!

Use Judgements to Steer Your Thinking Wider

This discernment versus judgement approach example may help you. I was travelling back late from a day's work many hours from my next work venue. I arrived at Manchester station very cold, very tired and realised on emerging from the station it was raining cats and dogs, great big wet ones! The hotel was just around the corner but far enough for me to get absolutely soaked. I dashed on feeling miserable, as I'd decided this was awful and then I realised if this wasn't okay for me, I could now start planning what was okay. I discerned that as soon as I got checked in at the hotel, I'd have a hot bath, room service and snuggle up in my bed. This immediately lifted my mood and took me out of the pity party that was building in my head and gave me plenty to run faster towards, out of the rain.

Despite This, Judgements Do Help Us

Drawing on past learning helps us focus too, helps us learn and get on with our day.

Forgive me for another weather analogy but I'm British, what do you expect? You need to go out and you quickly make a judgement on what you need to put on to do this; if you were just discerning, you'd have to think this through or even relearn the same thing that you learnt as a child. If it's raining you'll get wet, so take a coat and umbrella, If it's cold, wear a coat, more layers. We use previous learning and made those judgements a long time ago, going through the whole judgement process again is really a waste of time. These quick judgements generally serve us well and enable us to get on with our lives. The difficulty comes when the judgements come from the ego prodding us to measure ourselves against others. It's raining I wish I had a better coat, if I was better at..., I should be on holiday not working and so on.

Being Mindful of Our Internal Dialogue—Not Clearing, Stopping or Criticising

It is the nature of the mind to think; if you're not having thoughts then you're dead! Apologies if that's a bit too dramatic for you but it's true. Mindfulness or other meditation practices all do one thing. They direct the mind towards the breath, a neutral aspect or a mantra free of connotations, subtexts or personal stories. The KH1 Mb exercises, which I encourage you to use, allow you to develop the skill of directing the mind as you go about your everyday life.

Mb Exercises, Neuroplasticity and Teaching an Old Dog New Tricks!

The Mb exercises bring in calm and with that our ability to notice our thoughts and feelings, and we can use that space to decide if that thought is true for us or just a thought that can be left to come and go. We are constantly having thoughts and deciding which ones are important to us now. For example, "I would like to relax now rather than finish this, but I continue as the consequences do not suit me". Just as we aim to prioritise our thoughts, we can now get wise and select those thoughts that build our self-belief, confidence and well-being. Thoughts are not facts, they are just thoughts!

By noticing our thoughts rather than automatically engaging, we provide ourselves with space, space to choose the thoughts, feelings and emotions that are going to work in this time, at this point in our life, to boost and strengthen us. Other thoughts are free to come and go.

Standing on the Platform

Like trains coming into the station, we choose the train to get us to our chosen destination. Just because a train (thought) comes into the station we do not blindly get in it, we check first it is the one that will get us to where we want to go. If it is not, we let it pass us by and wait for the right train we choose. Just because a train (thought) comes in does not mean we have to get in it, we can just let it go and wait (create the right thoughts for us) for the right train, more likely to take us where we want to be: calm, confident and strong.

Know Too

We all have the ability to grow new neural (thinking) pathways, let old pathways fade away, and develop and pick new thinking habits and this ability is infinite. Our capacity to think in new ways, create new patterns of thinking, is not determined by our age, experience or intelligence. It is determined by our ability to notice and then choose. Proof positive that the old saying should be "you *can* teach an old dog new tricks", which is excellent news for us all.

I Know I Shouldn't, But I Can't Help It

Many of my clients say this to me and my answer is always the same. Actually, you can help it and divert to a more helpful thought, emotion, feeling and action, you just don't know *how* to yet. Thoughts are not facts—they are just thoughts—and you can pick better ones for you. If this is you wondering how, stop worrying about the how, just be willing to give it a go, to install Keeper Habit One and see what happens. What have you got to lose? You can carry on struggling or you can develop the skills to be who you want to be, both approaches demand the same level of energy. Use your stress, lack of confidence and so on to increase your feelings of calm and open the doors for you to freedom from all those downer thoughts and states. Do you want more stress for you or the ability to meet any challenges life gives you and really be free to choose and create what you want from life?

Let's Get Started

Remember, You Gain and Gain, Forget Try and Try

I suggest you start with the "Even Breath" Mb exercise, but it is up to you. Each Mb exercise will calm the chatter of the mind and enable you to focus on what you are doing now. The "Soothing Breath" Mb exercise calms down the body and the mind quickly so I tend to teach these two first to clients. I just wonder what do you do now, that's kind, to help maintain your focus or calm yourself down? Struggle, push yourself harder, beat yourself up verbally, mentally? You can use the Mb exercises almost anywhere and get results, just make sure it is safe for you to take your focus inwards and away from your surroundings. Obviously crossing the road is a no-no! The exercises are all explained at the end of this chapter with a weekly checklist to record your progress if you find that useful. The podcast links are also included below each exercise if you prefer listening while you get to know the Mb exercises. Choose the best approach for you.

Habit Tagging

To help you form Keeper Habit One, and any new habit, there is an easy technique to use. Say you want to use the "Even Breath" exercise three times a day. Think of something you do at least three times a day. An example could be having a cup of coffee or tea. From now on you, add onto that habit an "Even Breath" practice. In this way you use an existing routine or habit to build in a new one. This doesn't mean you cannot do an Mb exercise at any other time, maybe when you are feeling that mid-afternoon slump (one that frequently gets me). As for the "Soothing Breath" exercise, I would recommend you practise that whenever you have a break and just as you settle down for sleep each night. Now you know when and how to just do it, bring these simple, quick exercises into your day and feel the benefits from each exercise too. It really is that easy to start changing!

Successes and Achievements Diary—Your Journal

The Successes and Achievements Diary is designed to be just that, not something to beat yourself up with, or focus on what you have not done but to focus on what you have done. Remember you will miss or forget to do the exercises; just carry on, focus on when you remember and celebrate your progress. Whatever the pace is it's your pace, just your perfect. The important thing is to keep going and you are changing. Change is a gradual process not an instant process.

Plan to Program Your Mind

Use your diary to do a nightly review and plan for tomorrow. For example, which Mb exercise and number/frequency of exercises, when and patterns of thinking you will experiment with: positive, judgements and discernments. Doing this last thing at night before we go to sleep (using "Soothing Breath" if you like) actively programs your mind for tomorrow and helps you stick to your plans. You can also add on anything else you aim to do tomorrow.

Important Reminder

For all exercises make sure you are safe to focus inwards and defocus from your surroundings for a minute or two.

Keeper Habit One (KH1) Mb Exercises

Mb Exercise: Even Breath

This is a quick easy method. It boosts your focus, calms you down and brings you into the now. All in three breaths! This is a key tool for you and one you can use frequently. Added to that, it helps to grow the neural pathways to direct your attention, training your mind to do what you want. First, you defocus to allow yourself to refocus.

1. Get yourself in a comfortable, safe place. Relax your shoulders and sit or stand straight.
2. Either close your eyes or stare at a fixed point and focus on your breathing.
3. You can put your hands on your tummy to feel it rise and fall.
4. Breathe through your nose and count in your breath to the count of three (one, two, three) and pause. Now release your breath through your nose counting three, two, one and pause. Do this three times. Notice the breath coming in and out of your nose and filling your belly.

5. Now open your eyes, or focus back on your surroundings and come back to the present moment. Direct your focus to what you are doing.

https://fionachapmanspodcast.buzzsprout.com/1882592/9531133

Mb Exercise: Soothing Breath

Use your breath to calm the mind and soothe our natural stress reactor mechanism (more about that later). Remember you can do this anywhere and for those of you that have problems getting off to sleep, this has been reported by clients as really helpful.

1. Stop whatever you are doing and get yourself comfortable, relax your shoulders, straighten your back and either stand, sit or even lie down.
2. Become aware of your breathing and focus on the in breath and then the out breath.
3. Feel the breath going in through your nose, into your lungs, expanding your chest and pushing your tummy outwards.

4. Release the breath slowly out through your nose.
5. Now soothe the breath and on the in breath count to four.
6. Release your out breath through the nose to a slower pace of eight.
7. Breathe in to the count of four and out to the count of eight (or whatever feels comfortable so that the out breath is longer than your in breath).

https://fionachapmanspodcast.buzzsprout.com/1882592/9531186

It is perfectly natural for the mind to wander. The power is in you directing your mind back to focusing on the breath, building your ability to direct your mind.

Mb Exercise: Naming and Calming

This is a quick easy one to release stress when you notice it building in you. Take a moment to allow yourself to break out of the stress habit.

1. Get yourself in a comfortable, safe place. Relax your shoulders and sit or stand straight yet softly relaxed.

2. Either close your eyes or stare at a fixed point and focus on your breathing.
3. You can put your hands on your tummy to feel it rise and fall.
4. Breathe through your nose and count in your breath to the count of three (one, two, three) and pause. Now release your breath through your nose counting three, two, one and pause.
5. Allow your breathing to carry on naturally, open or refocus your eyes and move your head to the right, naming everything you see.
6. Slowly move your head from right to left and back to centre, naming everything you see either out loud or in your head.
7. Take one more deep breath and as you release it imagine releasing the last of any tension and refocus on what you were doing.

https://fionachapmanspodcast.buzzsprout.com/1882592/9612514

Mb Exercise: Self-Compassion

This exercise grows that self-love and support muscle, making it stronger than the judge or critic the more you do it. Every time you notice that inner voice giving you a hard time, use it as a springboard to grow your self-compassion. If you have any restricted movement in your arms you can adapt to the "hug" you can manage and still benefit from the exercise.

1. Get yourself in a comfortable, safe place. Relax your shoulders and sit or stand straight yet softly relaxed.
2. Take a few deep even breaths as you close your eyes or stare at a fixed point and focus on your breathing.
3. Wrap your arms around your body and give yourself a firm hug. Notice the sensations of being hugged.
4. Then gently rock yourself, just a tiny movement, and continue hugging.
5. When you are ready, release the hug a little and gently rub the top of your arms.
6. When you are ready, take a deep even breath and release your arms, open your eyes/refocus on your surroundings and come back into your now.

https://fionachapmanspodcast.buzzsprout.com/1882592/9579466

Mb Exercise: Toes and Feet

1. Get yourself in a comfortable, safe place. Relax your shoulders and sit or stand straight yet softly relaxed.
2. Take a few deep even breaths to ground you as you close your eyes or stare at a fixed point.
3. Now focus your attention on your toes and direct your attention to the little toe on your foot, either left or right. Really mentally explore the toe, notice how it feels and what is touching it and then move onto the next toe. You may find you need to wiggle some toes to help you connect with them and notice how it feels.
4. Explore each toe in the same way, working from right to left or left to right until you reach the final little toe on the opposite foot.
5. Take a deep even breath and open or refocus your eyes and come back into your now.

https://fionachapmanspodcast.buzzsprout.com/1882592/9531223

Mb Exercise: Sounds

1. Get yourself in a comfortable, safe place. Relax your shoulders and sit or stand straight yet softly relaxed.
2. Take a few deep even breaths to ground you as you close your eyes or stare at a fixed point.
3. Notice the sound furthest away from you. Once you locate it, just notice it, avoid labelling it, just really listen to that sound furthest away from you.
4. Just listen to the sound.
5. Then notice the sound closest to you. Again, just listen to it and allow yourself to just listen to the actual sound.
6. When you are ready, and if you have not done it already, focus on the sound of your breath. Listen to the sound.
7. Now take a deeper breath and open your eyes/refocus on your surroundings and come back into your now.

https://www.buzzsprout.com/1882592/episodes/9531212

Mb Exercise: Body Scanning

To do this body scan you do not have to follow the pathway described below but can travel in the general direction from toes to head in any way that suits you. This enables you to make the exercise however long or short you want it to be. Just notice the sensations, feelings in the body, avoiding any judgement. Just notice.

1. Get yourself in a comfortable, safe place. Relax your shoulders and sit or stand straight yet softly relaxed.
2. Take a few deep even breaths to ground you as you close your eyes or stare at a fixed point.
3. Notice how the tips of your toes feel and then the soles of your feet. Just explore and notice how they feel. Avoid judgements, such as good or bad, Just notice. Observe how your toes and feet feel.
4. Wiggle your toes and notice how your foot moves, what parts of the foot touch the ground/shoe or whatever they are resting on.
5. Travel up your legs and notice how wiggling your toes affects your legs, the muscles, how they move.

6. Now relax your toes and focus on your lower back and hips. Notice what they touch, how they feel, just notice. If you make judgements just notice and refocus your attention on the body part you are exploring for sensation awareness.
7. Move your attention to the mid and upper back and then shoulders. Noticing the feel and sensations as you explore these parts of your body.
8. Keep travelling up your body, exploring your stomach, chest and arms, hands until you reach your neck.
9. Explore your head, face, cheeks and jaw.
10. When you reach your scalp or wish to finish, just take a deep even breath and as you release it open/refocus your eyes and come back into the now.

https://fionachapmanspodcast.buzzsprout.com/1882592/9531151

Mb Exercise: Fingertips and Hands

1. Get yourself in a comfortable, safe place. Relax your shoulders and sit or stand straight yet softly relaxed.

2. Take a few deep even breaths to ground you as you close your eyes or stare at a fixed point.
3. Place the tips of your forefingers together and softly rub them together and notice the sensations. How does it feel? Smooth, rough, hard or soft? Just notice.
4. Then put all your fingertips together and continue to gently rub, noticing the sensations. Rub a bit harder and feel the ridges if you can.
5. Now place the palms together and gently rub and notice the sensations, the temperature.
6. Move your fingers over the back of your hands letting your fingertips explore the feel and sensations of the back of your hands.
7. When you are ready to come back into the now, just take a deep breath and on the out breath, open/refocus your eyes.

https://fionachapmanspodcast.buzzsprout.com/1882592/9531159

Daily Record of Exercises, Successes and Achievements!

Day	Mb exercise and number of repetitions	Saying it positively	Judgement vs discernment	Noticing internal dialogue/ feelings	Plans for tomorrow

Getting Ready for Keeper Habit Two

While you are getting into Keeper Habit One and allowing it to take root, remember, at your own pace, you can move on to Keeper Habit Two (KH2), which focuses on building your self-belief (your self-esteem and confidence), exploring what you really want for yourself, enabling your self-esteem to allow your confidence to flow and create what you want for you. Remember, you are bringing in new habits, a new way of thinking, so allow these habits to take root as you explore your wonderful potential and clear the fog of stress. Go at your own pace, celebrate what you do, notice when you achieve and allow that to be your focus—what you do, not what you do not do, or worse, think you should do!

Working the Habits Together

The three keeper habits work together. You are learning now, very possibly for the first time, how to use your mind to support you, so start getting familiar with and trying out Keeper Habit Two together with Keeper Habit One as part of the process. All is good. Every exercise gives, lowers the stress and starts building the wonder of you. (If you cringed then at my expression "the wonder of you", that is just a gap in your self-esteem showing and you can now start to fix it.) No perfects, no trying, just doing and focusing on doing and you will be amazed at how your life changes. Finally, be aware. Stress gobbles up all your energy and just leads to more stress, anxiety and worse, whereas the three keeper habits open your mind to really being your biggest fan and plenty of whatever you need, now and in the future nows. That is why you are bringing in these habits to be the natural you and leave behind the stress and anxiety trap of modern living.

Case Study

One of my clients was experiencing extreme levels of stress at work and found that they were beginning to focus on one person as the cause. That person seemed to be constantly scrutinising their work and decisions. In addition, this person was more senior, and the client began to feel their job security and capabilities to do the job were in question.

I asked my client to use the Mb exercises to lower the stress throughout the day and whenever they felt picked on by this senior member of the management team. After just a week of doing the exercises at least three times a day and whenever they felt stressed, the client reported they felt better, less stressed.

I now asked them to use the space of calm to pause and ask themselves: is this the only way to understand this situation? I reminded them they needed to focus within, to find a way of responding and thinking in a way that maintains their calm and builds their self-belief. We discussed possible ways of responding that the client felt would help them, their stress levels and manage the situation more positively. I reminded them that when we change our behaviour, others need to respond in a different way.

My client planned how they wished to respond to any scrutiny or perceived criticism. At our next session they reported rather than feeling stressed and frustrated they could discuss and share their views with the manager and felt their relationship had begun to change. They reported it was early days but felt so much more positive about work and their ability to develop a more positive relationship with the manager. They doubted they would ever be best friends but had begun to think they could work together.

Key Takeaways

How to get Keeper Habit One installed:

- The exercises build your capacity to notice stress as it arises and reduce its impact.
- Use the mindfulness-based (Mb) exercises to lower stress and grow a calm habit.
- Record and focus on what you do, forget what you forgot. Focus on your daily progress doing the exercises, your successes and achievements.
- Start using Keeper Habit Two with Keeper Habit One.

Further Reading and Listening

Audio versions of the Mb exercises can also be located on my podcast Fiona Chapman's Podcast @thechapwellmethod (buzzsprout.com). You will also find the audio version of this book there to support you.

The Zen Monkey and the Lotus Flower: 52 Stories to Relieve Stress, Stop Negative Thoughts, Find Happiness, and Live Your Best Life by Tenpa Yeshe,

Emotional Intelligence Unleashed: Transform Your Life with Proven NLP Strategies to Manage Stress, Improve Communication Skills and Achieve Personal Growth by Jon Manning

The Body Keeps the Score: Brain, Mind, and Body in the Healing of Trauma by Bessel van der Kolk

CHAPTER 3

Building Unshakeable Self-Belief

Cultivate the mindset of confidence and resilience to overcome challenges and unlock your full potential.

Keeper Habit Two: Keep Self-Belief High

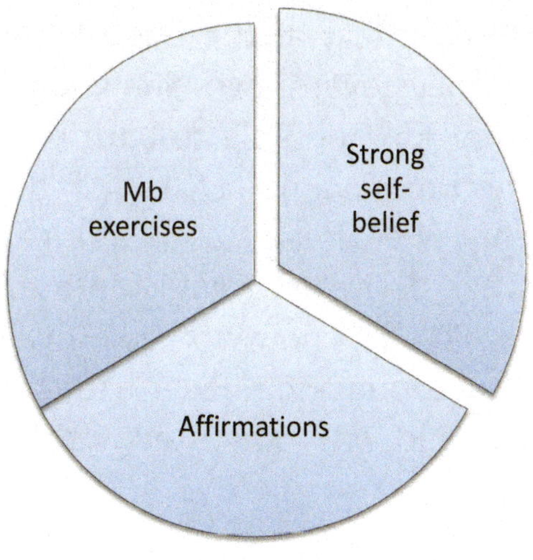

Repairing and Strengthening Self-Belief = Confidence and Self-Esteem

Keep going with your chosen Keeper Habit One exercises while you start to explore your self-belief, self-esteem and confidence working effectively together. The exercises in Keeper Habit One not only lower the fog of stress but also create the space for you to build your self-belief, repair any gaps that will hold you back, generate more stress, drain your confidence and leave you settling for less.

Case Study: Affirmations Manifesting Your Best Life

A client came to me wanting to handle money better, to earn enough to be able to relax more and do more of the things she wanted. Every time she earned more, she found it was not enough and in fact at the end of the month she was always overdrawn. She knew she was good at her job and able to earn money, but she wanted more time for herself, her family and so on. She already used affirmations to support her desire to create more money in her life, which she knew worked. However, this client always found she never had enough for everything and was exhausted and frustrated with herself despite her career success and growing ability to increase her earnings.

We did some work together and her affirmations were totally focused on her goal and met all the requirements of affirmations to support goal achievement. There was a big gap though; she had totally neglected her self-belief, self-esteem and confidence. On further exploration, she did not believe in her own worth to have money, to be able to work and yet have time to enjoy other things too. Her affirmations were powerful in focusing her attention on creating wealth, but they were in direct conflict with her self-belief and all those things she had learnt about money.

Hard work is the only way to earn money, relaxation is laziness, people like us do not get rich, more money than sense, money is short, money does not come easily, life is hard. Her self-esteem and confidence with money was founded on these sayings and though most could be tracked back to who taught them to her, all it shows is that her teacher had the same problem, and it was all they could teach her.

Forget blaming or looking for someone to blame. Any change or goal you desire needs to include building your self-belief philosophy to ensure you truly believe you deserve what you desire. My client needed to make sure her self-belief fully supported her desires and needs, aligning her self-esteem and confidence to match what she wanted for herself internally and externally. Often, affirmation and manifestation work are taught as separate to our inner selves, focused on our outer world but if we do not do the internal work our self-belief will always scupper our achievements. My client started including affirmations about deserving money, fun and relaxation. She also used Keeper Habit One to increase her self-awareness of her thoughts, feelings and actions that were pushing money away.

For example, she noticed she would shop and buy things she liked but did not need or even really want. She began to consider her intended purchases in a different way. Do I want these or my goal? I can have these, but I will need to work longer, is this okay with me? Do I want to push money away or bring it in? Things changed very rapidly for her after that realisation and enabled her to change her behaviour with money. Her self-belief in deserving and being worthy of "having enough money" accelerated her ability to manage her money to achieve her goal and enjoy money rather than feeling it was a battlefield!

Manifesting = Affirmations and Goals Focused on the Internal Needs

Often, we decide what we want and then focus on the external world to achieve it. The achievement of any goal needs to match our inner desires and needs. Happiness comes from meeting our needs, our inner needs, and then reflecting our inner world outwards. When setting any goals and building your affirmations always make sure you focus 20 per cent on the external goal and 80 per cent on building your self-belief in your deservedness of whatever you decide you want and need.

Case Study

One of my clients constantly talked about how important his family was to him and being a good father. However, he could only remember how his own father acted and was determined to be different. Consequently, he found time with his children stressful and exhausting as he was focused on being a perfect father. We discussed what a good father was to him and what sort of a person he was, his likes and dislikes. Through this discussion he developed a picture of how he wanted to be and feel as a father.

He then built five affirmations to support his goal of spending more time with his children:

I am loving, loved and lovable within my family

I have fun being with my family

I can relax just being me with my children

My family time allows me to be myself

I am a good father

Self-Confidence and Self-Esteem

As we wake up each day, we have all the confidence we need. However, it's kept in our self-esteem container and if there are holes or gaps, your self-confidence leaks right through or even gushes! Alongside that, our self-esteem containers have compartments and some of those sections have no holes while others have a range of gaps. For the purpose of working with yourself, you need to realise you always have confidence; it's how much leakage is going through your self-esteem container that causes the problem.

The good news is when we know how we can fix those holes, gaps, with affirmations. We have all the confidence we need.

Where's Your Lack Right Now?

Notice the area of your life where you feel a lack of confidence, the need to change, improve, or where you feel stuck. By doing this, you allow yourself to explore who you really are capable of being, fully rounded and comfortable in all areas of your life, balanced. You don't need to work on every area or even one. It's just about knowing your strengths and weaknesses, so you are able to address them if and when they get in your way. It's like being able to run a marathon before doing any training. You train specifically to run a marathon and if you're not planning to run a marathon why would you use your time training for a marathon? This checking in with ourselves on a regular basis helps us know where we need to internally grow to achieve a specific goal, to meet a need. Soley focusing on the external goal neglects the real work, preparing internally for our goal so we are able to use and spot the external opportunities to achieving our goal and feeling the satisfaction of achievement. This approach to building our life releases the stress and struggle and allows us to meet our needs and desires using our natural strengths and talents.

Real World, Not Pretend World

It's also about being realistic and really, really comfortable with our self-belief needs and adjusting to keep them satisfied. Not everyone is everything, but everyone has everything they need.

Exploring your self-belief is about finding out how you think about yourself, how you value yourself and what you believe you deserve, deep down versus what you need.

The formula for all of us is simple:

Inner world = self-esteem and confidence = our self-belief + you in the outer world

Regular Check-Ups

You can explore your self-esteem for any gaps draining your never-ending confidence flow using the Quick Self-Esteem Checker exercise below. Find out where you are at the moment and where you can strengthen yourself. Be aware our self-esteem is not static; strong self-esteem can stay strong, most of the time, but in challenging times in our life, or when we are feeling vulnerable, we can feel it wobble and then it is important to confidently boost it back. That is true resilience, the ability to boost ourselves back to well-being. Be alert to when you need extra care and give it to yourself with love, fixing that gap, not allowing it to grow. Understand our humanity is an opportunity to grow and look after ourselves. Understand, too, the whole range of feelings and emotions are what it is to be human, not right or wrong, just human. It is your ability to bounce back, look after yourself, that matters and to repair any gaps. Our resilience is our responsibility and only we can maintain it for ourselves when we understand how.

Keeper Habit Two (KH2) Exercises

Exercise: Quick Self-Esteem Checker

Start this exercise by using your favourite Mb exercise, helping you to relax, clear your mind and feel safe. Be honest. This is about you, never perfection. Being true to you is your perfection, constantly looking after and building your strength and resilience. We are keeping you strong and resilient so there is plenty to spare in the tougher and more challenging times which, in general, we are all likely to experience at some time or other.

Statement		**Score 1 to 5** 1 not at all, 2 sometimes, 3 frequently, 4 mostly, 5 always
I always value and appreciate myself. I'm okay and matter.	A	
I think well of myself. I'm okay.	A	
I treat myself well and look after myself most of the time.	A	
I accept myself, all of me.	A	
I consider my good points, talents, skills, qualities and my not-so-good points make up my uniqueness, make up me!	A	
I feel good about myself all the time.	A	
Total Area A points (max 30)		
I feel I deserve other people's attention, time and help.	C	
I feel confident asking for others' help.	C	
I enjoy looking after and treating myself. I'm worth it.	C	
I believe I deserve the best life.	C	

I believe I am worthy of success.	C	
I expect of myself the same as I expect of others.	C	
Total area C points (max 30)		
I recognise I am human and quickly recover from everyday setbacks (e.g. being late, missing a connection, burning a meal, forgetting something).	B	
I find it easy to ask for help when I need it.	B	
My self-talk is always encouraging and supportive no matter how challenging things may be or how many mistakes I make.	B	
I allow myself enough time to learn new habits, knowledge, ways of doing things.	B	
I like learning and finding out new things.	B	
I like doing new things and going to new places.	B	
Total area B points (max 30)		

For this exercise imagine your self-esteem has three parts: A, B and C. This approach helps us navigate and provide our personalised self-care diet, no matter what is happening for us.

Separate your scores into each area of your self-esteem.

Area of self-esteem	**Points out of 30**
As are all about your self-image, self-perception, self-concept: overall image, view of yourself, your self-worth.	
Bs are all about your self-efficacy, self-acceptance: how well you perceive you can do things, adapt, learn.	
Cs are all about your self-respect, self-worth: how you value yourself, opinions and beliefs about yourself	

Now you can find out where you are stronger and where you may be feeling a bit vulnerable, lacking confidence, or losing confidence through a gap and most likely compensating with stress too frequently (remember good stress, if released, is fine) to get you through.

If you scored 26 to 30 your self-esteem has firm foundations in this area with very few "gaps". It's likely you recover quickly from any challenges and stresses. We can all have moments of self-doubt or times when we are feeling not as strong, and this is normal. Maybe right now, you are recovering from an illness or disappointment, or times are challenging, and this brings our self-esteem under attack. Being aware of your needs and how to "Mind Your Gap" between well-being and stress is important to ensure you remain mentally strong, resilient now and throughout your life. Getting a lower score in any area is not right or wrong, merely an indicator of a gap that will leak your confidence just when you need it most.

Let Your Self-Awareness Be Your Guide

As you begin to be more attuned to your needs you will know what and which scores are okay for the powerful uniqueness of you. I am starting you off to explore how you feel at set points between 26 to 30. As you gain experience you will know what works best for you and your life, so please confidently choose for you as you gain experience in your personal self-care needs. These scores are not designed to measure yourself against but merely to choose the perfect mind diet for you and the life you choose.

Working on What You Need Rather Than Stressing

If you are not feeling a lack of confidence, not feeling a struggle, why would you worry about it? It is all about knowing how to find and sort any gaps once you spot the struggle or recognise a challenge that will require your self-esteem and confidence to stay strong. Maybe you find you are struggling, yet scored 26 or more, then you can maintain the strength using affirmations making sure your confidence and self-esteem continue to support you at the exact time you need it.

If you scored between 20 and 26 your self-esteem tends to vary depending on what situation you are in and what is happening in your life. It is normal for our self-esteem to be variable, we are human, and throughout our lives we experience a range of challenges; some we choose, some we get. Knowing how to boost yourself, take control of your inner world, and knowing when and how is key to your success and resilience.

If you scored lower than 20 it is likely your self-esteem is leaking your self-confidence frequently and limiting your choices and life experience. Alongside that your mental resilience reserve will be too low, and you could be vulnerable to the negative impact of too much stress running for too long and too high leading to low mood, anxiety and even physical ailments.

Let Go of Pass or Fail, Good or Bad

Scores are not a pass or fail situation or good or bad, they are an information-gathering exercise for you to know yourself more. The more self-aware you are, the more you can look after yourself and guide yourself towards maintaining calm strength, plenty of resilience reserves and flow with life. If you find yourself tempted to classify your score as good or bad, needs improvement, then remind yourself self-awareness is your aim, understanding where you are at the moment and taking action to strengthen you in your now and your future nows is more important. There is no right or wrong, there is only growth. Understand both success and failure are our teachers, nothing more, nothing less. The critic habit is the trap that just generates stress.

Exercise: Your Self-Esteem—Pulling It all Together

Imagine you are in a coaching conversation with me now. I just wonder what you would say. Is your confidence low or is it your self-esteem, both or neither? In every situation in your life are you the same? Or do you seem better in some situations than others? Me, for example, I am strong and confident at work but sometimes, out of work, shyness can bubble up. Just reflect on those areas where you are confident and where you can benefit with a bit more confidence, as that is the part of your self-esteem where the gap is allowing your confidence quota to flow away rather than flow for you.

Make Some Notes Here or in Your Journal

Do this exercise over a few days to gather a more rounded understanding of yourself in a range of situations and times.

I feel most confident in the following situations and places:

____

____

I feel less confident in the following situations and places:

Now reflect back on your self-esteem exercise and consider which areas are working well for you and which areas can be repaired, strengthened, noting any gaps that need healing to allow you to access your confidence fully. Allow your confidence to be there for you rather than flowing through a gap. Make some notes here.

Not Just Affirmations

This section is focusing on using affirmations. I wanted to remind you how self-care also includes a rounded approach. Look back over your notes on your confidence levels over the last few days and consider if some needed other aspects of self-care such as rest, good food, fun, sleep, exercise, good company and so on. The balance is complex and unique to you. Me, for example, I feel much better if I have had enough sleep or rest and affirmations will give me a boost, but they do not mitigate my need for rest!

Affirmations to Suit Your Gaps

Having established you need to do some self-care in terms of your self-esteem and confidence the first technique is a constant technique that you will use daily. I suggest you start by adding them onto every Mb exercise you do—after each Mb exercise, repeat your affirmations. Affirmations become our daily diet to boost us and keep us mentally strong. Just as we take care of ourselves physically on a daily basis, we also need to use the same approach for the mind. As you work your way through this book you are acquiring many ways to help your mind stay strong, support you, and the combination of Mb exercises and affirmations directs your mind to support you.

The TEA Model: How the Mind Works

Our mind works like this: we have a thought (T) which gives us an emotion/feeling (E) which leads us to act (A). To build up or shrink any part of our mind to get the balance we need, want and choose to support us, we need to go within, notice, be aware of what our minds are doing, which thoughts, feelings we are acting on, and use that understanding as a springboard for change, never criticism. Thoughts are never facts, they are just thoughts that generate feelings, emotions, which then lead us to act. Get picky and choose thoughts that boost, repair gaps, not create gaps and damage.

We either make ourselves happy or miserable. The amount of work is the same.

Carlos Castaneda

Pick Your Five a Day

Based on your reflections and on your scores, pick the affirmations to meet your needs, your unique needs and gaps that are leaking your confidence and drawing on stress to try to fill them. To generally maintain your self-esteem just pick a selection from each area. Try to pick no more than five to six because you need to be able to easily remember them and if you pick more than that you are likely to forget.

Area of self-esteem	Affirmation examples
The A section is all about our self-image, self-perception, self-concept: overall image, view of yourself, your self-worth.	I am beautiful, stunning, gorgeous inside and out I am worth more than I believe I deserve the very best What I desire matters I have everything I need to achieve my desires I am enough I am loving, lovable and loved I enjoy my uniqueness with love I am safe and comfortable living my best life I am strong I am happy in my own skin
The B section is all about our self-efficacy, self-acceptance: how well we perceive we can do things, adapt, learn.	I am capable I am efficient, capable and talented I flow through life with ease I learn easily I am adaptable, flexible and able I flow/progress at the perfect pace I am able to create the life I desire I am open to new things and change Change is a part of my successful life I respond to life with ease I confidently accept help I deserve help

The C section is all about our self-respect, self-worth: value of ourselves, opinions and beliefs about ourselves.	I truly value every part of me, all the time I trust myself I am enough I love myself I am free to be me I am safe I am needed I make decisions to meet my strengths I am enough now and always I accept myself and allow my strengths and weaknesses to be a welcome part of me I choose the best for me with love I am a gift Negative feelings always fade away, good feelings last Negative feelings never last I can see the light at the end of the tunnel There is always a light at the end of the tunnel. Nothing stays the same, everything changes. Everything is okay, everything will be okay.

Affirmations and How They Help You Reprogram Your Self-Belief

Remembering that by self-belief I mean your combined self-esteem and confidence flow. Repeat these affirmations regularly as you go about your day and especially after you do a Mb exercise or feel challenged. You will learn more about how to use the power of affirmations in Keeper Habit Three. For now just bring them in to boost you on this magnificent journey to access the power of you and heal the gaps.

Affirmation Design Tips

You can either use the examples above, design your own specific affirmations or modify the ones given.

Create your affirmations to conform to the rules of affirmations.

Affirmations must be:

- in the present tense, as if happening now, or if it feels easier use words such as "I am beginning to", "gradually I am feeling", etc.
- in your language (you can adapt the words to suit you)
- worded to only state the positive

- not too long otherwise you may forget them and no more than five to seven as a maximum. If you are forgetting them, then you have too many.

Move Them Around

The examples I have given above can be moved around to suit you. Maybe using "I am okay" works better for you in the section for self-acceptance/efficacy and that is good. The important point is the affirmations mean something to you and the repairing/boosting of your self-esteem.

Case Study: Changing from Stress to Success

One of my recent clients, a successful fitness trainer and coach, particularly specialised in getting people fit for a challenge such as a marathon. My client started working as a fitness coach three years ago following a debilitating bout of depression and as part of his recovery, fitness and physical training were very important to him. His life now is very different, and he repeatedly said he enjoyed his work, had a good relationship and his own place. All the things he wanted he had achieved yet he couldn't understand why he was always worrying about things. Consequently he was very worried his depression was coming back or going to return sooner or later. He tried to stop worrying but it just seemed to get worse. To help him, I explained by trying to stop thoughts he was fully focusing on them and in fact, giving them more strength.

The trick is to notice your thoughts and feelings, shift your attention into neutral by labelling a thought and then inserting a better, more helpful thought. Using the Mb exercises my client reduced his stress and increased his ability to notice the worry thoughts and feelings. When he noticed he was worrying, he would mentally label it "worry thought" or "stress feeling" and bring in the previously prepared affirmations that helped to repair that gap in his self-esteem.

The Mb exercises continue to lower your stress and increase your capacity to notice the thoughts and feelings that trigger those stressful, worry feelings. When you notice these thoughts and feelings, you can direct your mind to choose better for you, your affirmations, rather than get stuck in unhelpful thinking and feeling patterns.

Neuroplasticity: Changing Thought Patterns

By noticing unhelpful thought patterns or stressful feelings, you can change by using those thoughts and feelings as an opportunity to bring in a more helpful thought pattern, an affirmation. Every time you use stress thoughts or feelings to bring in your affirmations you will be building a new thinking, feeling way of being. Building yourself up. We have the ability to grow new thought habits forever! Often, we are unaware of the thought patterns we use as they are buried deeply in our unconscious programming but we always notice the feeling. You can use either the thought or feeling making you uncomfortable that can be reprogrammed in this way.

Do you already know some of your unhelpful thoughts?

- Do you criticise yourself?
- Do you look in the mirror and dislike what you see?
- Do you worry?
- Do you expect the worst?
- Do your everyday sayings reinforce the negative side of life or the positive?
- Do you "mind read" and think you know what people think?

- Do you always think of the worst-case scenario first?
- Is it half-full or half-empty for you?

Start Your Success and Achievements Journal

I always ask clients to start a journal and make its title My Success and Achievements Journal, as they begin working towards creating a stress-free life full of the things they did not even realise they wanted and needed plus the wonderful things they choose to bring into their life. I recommend you start your journal now if you have not already. If you are someone who prefers an IT approach, set up a file now, make it colourful and something you see immediately every time you log on. If, like me, you opt for a paper version, choose something beautiful, a journal that you enjoy using, happy to leave out so you see it, use it every day and it becomes a record of your success and achievements for now and for future use too. I use mine daily, reminding me to look after my inner world and how best to do that plus how and what I want to create for me.

Audit Your Thinking Patterns

Maybe you can recognise some of your thinking habits, or maybe you can add to your list of habits. Take a moment to reflect on your patterns of thinking.

In your Success and Achievements Journal make two columns, head each column positive and negative, and list the sayings, thoughts you frequently use, including the helpful ones and those that may be fear-based thinking. Neither column is right or wrong, they are either positive or negative; it is up to you which thoughts you recognise create your "feel-good" strength and allow your confidence to flow. As you become aware of your thinking habits you can then choose which to keep and which to consciously replace. Recognise it is not the world that is worrying you but actually your response to things, your inner world.

Using Your Journal of Successes and Achievements

When you journal, avoid just making it a retelling of your day, your woes! Make your journal a reflection of what worked for you today, focus on what went well. There will be plenty of things that have worked out okay for you; reflect and focus on the good, successful parts of your day, however minor. Start to recall the thoughts and feelings you experienced when things went well. What you focus on you get more of and by reflecting at the end of the day like this you are programming your mind for the successes of tomorrow. These thoughts and feelings can be minor; someone helped me as I struggled through the door, my coffee/tea tasted delicious. Get used to programming yourself for success rather than distress.

Take One Thing to Work On

When you reflect on your day, the focus is on what worked for you and reflecting on how well you are doing, building you up not bringing you down. If you wish you can choose just one thing that you feel could have gone better for you after you have explored your successes. Highlighting and focusing on your successes helps you to grow this part of your day. What you focus on you get more of, so if anything could have gone better for you, focus on how to improve things and the actions, thoughts and feelings you can use to make this happen. No judgements, no criticisms just growth, learning and improvement. Use the Growth Triggers Question Set to start exploring how to start creating what you want more of next time an opportunity arises.

What situation would I like to improve?

Step 1 What are my thoughts around this? *Away from the situation? Before the situation? During the situation? After the situation?*

Step 2 What are my feelings about this? *Away from the situation? Before the situation? During the situation? After the situation?*

Step 3 What were my actions? *What did I say, do, act like? Before the situation? During the situation? After the situation?*

Throughout the exercise remind yourself of the "in my control" and "out of my control" rules (Chapter 1) and how you can only make any real impact in the "in my control" area.

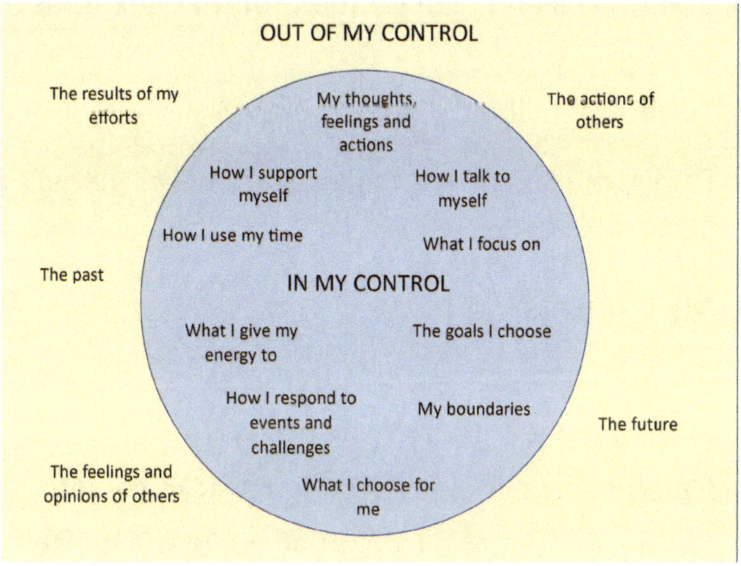

And then rewrite it to get the outcome you prefer for next time. Review those thoughts and feelings and actions to match your preferred outcome for you, not changing anyone else, just you and your experience in your inner world. To create the inner world for you in that situation, focus on the thoughts, feelings and actions you would experience/do if you experienced the situation/event as you want.

Start with something small, doable and try to be as honest with yourself as possible. This is an example kindly donated from a recent client. Notice it does not need to be perfect. Notice, too, how the reverse brainstorm technique helped this client open up her thinking. It is most important to give yourself time to adopt the new approach and do not look for perfection, ever. Reflect in your journal on the things that went well and plan for more of that next time!

Situation (I would like to improve)

Family mornings first thing before we all go our separate ways

My thoughts

I'm tired and got so much to do

They/he/she are just being awkward

Everyone else is always trying to make me late

He/she does not help get us all out of the house on time

My feelings

Frustration

Irritation rising to anger

Impatience

Resentment

My actions

Start shouting as soon as I get up

Start rushing and telling everyone to hurry up

Moving fast, apt to drop things, be clumsy

Situation (rewrite with a different outcome for next time)

Family mornings first thing before we all go our separate ways to be calmer and friendly

My thoughts

I am gradually feeling more awake and rested as I get dressed

They/he/she need reminding to do each thing/ ask for their help as they are so young/just focused on their own routine and do not know there is limited time/if I need help

Everyone else has things to do today the same as me

He/she/they can help get us all out of the house on time in their own way

I am relaxing into the morning routine, hiccups and all

My feelings (reverse brainstorm approach to this is recommended)

If not frustrated, I want to be calm

If not irritated, I want to be relaxed

If not impatient, I want to feel okay about any delays, repeated instructions to the younger ones, treat them as just the normal morning routine

Resentment

My actions

As I get dressed, just focus on me and start once I feel ready, make sure I get up with enough time to do this. Focus on relaxing my body as I get ready

Make some affirmations for me to repeat once I am ready to start the morning routine

Start shouting as soon as I get up: My body, mind and voice remain focused yet relaxed in the mornings

Start rushing and telling everyone to hurry up: Adopt a mindful approach and focus on each task fully as I do it

Moving fast, apt to drop things, be clumsy: Keep my movements relaxed yet purposeful and fluid

Affirmations

I am relaxed

I am able to remind people as much as is needed

I am looking forward to the day

I am focused and have enough time

You could even use anchoring to help you get into the different mindset that is more supportive to what you want to achieve.

Grow a Happiness Anchor

Sometimes we wake up feeling a bit low, not our usual self, and we notice our mood is low. This could be for many reasons. Maybe you had a tricky conversation yesterday that didn't go well. Maybe you're tired, or you overslept and then the rest of the day felt slightly off, out of step, or you ate too many rich foods yesterday. There can be all sorts of reasons for a low mood. We all have them; low mood days are being human and so is confidence and a strong sense of self-worth!

Are You a "Bad Day Believer"?

Or maybe something went wrong in your day and rather than fix it, get over it or forget it, your negative bias is now searching for more bad things to reinforce an old habit of yours. This is a thinking habit a lot of people have; that is, if one thing goes wrong it's going to be a "bad day". Then having programmed our minds to this fact, we start hunting for evidence, only noticing what goes wrong, overlooking anything that may contradict this fact. After all we are always right, aren't we? The temptation to be right rather than feel easier can become a habit! This exercise helps us lift our mood and nudge the mind back into a better, more helpful mood, a touch of the only way is up, not down.

Creating a "Feel-Good" Anchor

https://soundcloud.com/user-135417655/feel-good-anchor-mtg/s-Otoi8aLuRFC?si=49914245b40a4b308bf93c99cc274209&utm_source=clipboard&utm_medium=text&utm_campaign=social_sharing

A "feel-good" anchor is like installing a switch in your mind which you can switch on to feeling good; maybe it's happiness for you or feeling more positive and hopeful about things. By having a technique to boost yourself you can add to your resilience and coping mechanisms too. Think about it, when you're feeling good, happier, content—whatever you want to call it—you also feel more able to cope. Added to that you are more inclined to see your problems as smaller, less important, at least not so all-encompassing.

Anchors Away

To create your feel-good anchor, you maximise the good things in your life and make them work for you beyond the good moment. The more you explore the memory and feelings, the more your mind will get used to producing those feel-good, mood-uplifting responses just by bringing a mere flicker of the memory or thought patterns. It only takes a few minutes to do, the more you practise it, the deeper the habit forms. The good thing about growing this anchor or new thinking habit is you gain that feel-good boost every time you practise and build it into your mind. We'll use anchors a bit more throughout the book, so it helps to just think of them as setting up a rope to tug on the feel-good/easier feeling.

Exercise: Tugging Your Anchor

Just to be clear, you are not pretending all is well when there are things in your life that are not working for you; what you are doing is allowing a helpful frame of mind to support you. The problem may be minor, a lack of sleep, which you can fix in a few days, or it might be bigger, and you just have to work with it for now. Either way an easier frame of mind will help you enjoy the good things, too, and strengthen you to work through any challenges.

1. Make sure you are safe to close your eyes and focus inward. If you find closing your eyes difficult just stare at a fixed point. That's fine too.
2. Now pull up a memory of when you felt happy, content, safe. All those or just one is fine. It could have been an event, or listening to music, a person (if a person, choose someone who is in your life now), anything your mind gives you. If you struggle, just start creating your perfect day in your mind.
3. Imagine you are in that memory or perfect day, feel the feelings linked with your good memory or perfect day. Really feel them in your mind, your body and even your breath.

4. When you feel yourself smiling, enjoying those good feelings. You are noticing what feeling good is like for you. Enjoy it and revel in those feelings and thoughts. Imagine doubling them so they are bigger.
5. After a few minutes come back into the now bringing those feelings with you.
6. Refocus on whatever you are doing.

The more you do this exercise, the quicker you find yourself able to exercise that golden pot of feel-good. Why wouldn't you learn to tap into it?

Here are some more ways to really use journalling to build you up and create your personal journal of successes and achievements:

Exercises that work well for you: Oftentimes as we start to feel stronger, we forget to use or do not need certain exercises, and this is usual. Keeping a record of the exercises that work for you is helpful and a good idea, so you can easily use them and support yourself when you feel any struggles or dips in mood and need a bit of extra help. Your journal then becomes your personalised toolkit. Life is a flow, an ongoing growth process, and your journal helps you keep your life tools to hand, easy to access when you need them most. Remember you are never broken or weak.

There is just a gap in your knowledge on how to do "you" and now you can safely fill that gap.

Reflecting and redoing exercises: As you change and grow your confidence and self-esteem, your needs will also change, and gaps that never bothered you before may become evident. The journal provides an important record of what works, what you have achieved and how to easily keep yourself strong. This helps by allowing you to grow and develop throughout your life and use your past development as a guide and support for your future development needs.

Daily gratitude: Write three things that went well for you today. There will be at least three things, probably more. Our negative bias, if running too high, can block our memory and only focus on the bad things. This regular exercise helps you reset from a high negative bias to a more reasonable, balanced bias. If at first you can only think of one, start with that! Be kind to yourself, your starting point is perfect for you.

Your future plans: Write about how you'll be, feel, what you'll want, what you will be able to do, be, want then and so on. I encourage you to explore beyond your future goals to know for sure they are right for you. More about setting your future goals can be found in Chapter 5.

Today's discernments: Finish the sentence: I found out I prefer...

Today's judgements: Could they now become discernments?

Triggers: What happened? How can you use this trigger next time to develop what you want rather than repeat unsatisfactory patterns using the Growth Triggers Question Set?

What situation would I like to improve?

> **Step 1** What are my thoughts around this? *Away from the situation? Before the situation? During the situation? After the situation?*
>
> **Step 2** What are my feelings about this? *Away from the situation? Before the situation? During the situation? After the situation?*
>
> **Step 3** What were my actions? *What did I say, do, act like? Before during after the situation?*

Planning to respond in a different way is important and equips you to begin to experiment, increases mental flexibility and by interrupting responses with a Mb exercise, you can start to break down those unwanted patterns of behaviour, thoughts and feelings.

Positive things people have said to you/kindnesses you have accepted and given. Both minor and major, all matter from receiving and giving thank yous throughout the day to making it to that appointment on time. It is important to receive kindnesses as much as to give, it encourages the flow of life and abundance.

Achievements from small to bigger, all are achievements. Depending on where you are in your life, getting out of bed can be a success, making it to the school gates on time or presenting to a group. All are things to celebrate. By starting to focus on achievements you are programming your mind for success. Aim to record at least five a day, big or little, and do not forget the just-started first steps towards something bigger, it is all an achievement. Expecting success, celebrating success becomes a norm, which norm would you prefer? Some things will not work out how you planned. Learn to respond with curiosity and seeing the outcome, though different, as something new to explore rather than judge.

Curious Mind Question Set

Use the Curious Mind Question Set to explore any setbacks or unexpected outcomes to make them learning events, positives never failures, just preparation to go again and do something different, slightly or mostly to get what you want. What you used to call failures, disappointments become the stepping stone for you to achieve what you really want. Only accept growth answers to the question sets. They will be there, even if that way did not work!

1. What can I learn from this?
2. What have I discovered, know now that I did not know before?
3. What was positive about this?
4. How can I do this differently?
5. What was easy?
6. What was difficult?
7. How can I think kindly about this, myself?

Doing It Mindfully! Keeping Your Journal

Aim to spend time on your Success and Achievements Journal every evening or at least most evenings. Remember journalling at the end of each day and planning for tomorrow helps program your mind to remember and carry on when you wake up.

Reflecting, Accepting and Improving

Get used to reflecting on what you have done that day and plan to do the next day. Are today's exercises useful tools you will keep using or not? See what they feel like for you. Are they easy to do? Did they improve how you felt, thought about things, coped? How can you use them in the future? Add your comments at the end of each day, make notes, what works for you, what doesn't, what will keep you experimenting with them too. You are now building your capacity to be in tune with what is happening in your mind, building your resilience by noticing and observing you, then choosing what you want your mind to do for you, showing your mind how to support you and boost you. Any positive focus on you is like growth for your inner self-belief, so no criticisms, just information and choice going forward.

Learning to Notice: Observe Those Thoughts or Feelings/Emotions

As you develop your natural ability to notice and observe feelings, thoughts, emotions and actions you can ask yourself, does that help me, does it work for me, what would work for me, what would boost me now, rather than drag me down. Keep your regular Mb exercises going, as they will continue to grow your ability to notice your thoughts and make the choices that suit you, work for you. A thought or feeling is just a thought or feeling, not a fact. It is up to you to decide if it is true for you.

Let Yourself off the Hook

Get out of the habit of beating yourself up; use a carrot rather than a stick to bring in these changes. I have deliberately asked you to choose the exercises to suit you and make notes about your progress. Focus on what works for you. This approach makes your journey as unique as you. It is highly likely you will forget to do some of the exercises; focus on remembering and congratulate yourself when you remember. Avoid being hard on yourself when you forget, which you will, it is normal, but when you remember it is an opportunity for change, so celebrate those moments.

Spin Positive

Start noticing every time you criticise yourself and turn it into a positive. For example, you might forget something, or get something wrong, misjudge a situation, or any of these minor errors. Start noticing how you talk to yourself. Do you call yourself names or instead encourage yourself to let it go, encourage yourself to have another go now you've found out how not to do something for the result you want? Start paying attention to the self-talk and act like you were talking to your best friend in the most supportive way.

Spinning Positive in Your Journal

Use your journal to help you start tackling that inner critic if it is an issue for you. First you write down what sort of inner critic thoughts and sayings came up for you during the day. Draw a line down the middle of your page and in one column list all the critical things you have said and thought that day. Then in the second column write what your best friend would say to you instead. By writing and focusing on changing the inner critic for your best friend you are supporting and preparing to change from negative to spinning positive. Next time you notice your inner critic, you ask, what would my best friend say?

For example:

Inner critic	**Best friend**
You were useless	Well done for starting. That is the only way you will improve: practice!
What makes you think you will be any good at this?	You will learn and improve the more you do it. You've learnt loads of things before. It takes time!

Change Something in Your Routine

Change something that is a usual pattern for you. I suggest to clients the best one is to move the kettle in the kitchen. Or perhaps change something in your morning routine. For example, if you get dressed after having a drink or breakfast, get dressed first and then have your drink or breakfast. By changing a routine, you take yourself out of autopilot into task-positive mode. Basically, autopilot is your experience when you are miles away, not even aware of what you are doing. Task-positive mode is being fully in the now. Taking yourself out of autopilot can feel a bit uncomfortable. By doing it with simple things you learn how to look after yourself and support yourself by saying nice things to yourself when you find yourself unwittingly autopiloting old habits. You are increasing your ability to be self-aware, which is where change happens.

Practise Feeling Good

For this exercise take some time to remember a really happy memory. Keep revisiting that memory throughout the day. Take a minute to imagine you are back there right in the memory, feel the feelings you had, let them fill your mind and body. Bring yourself back to the now. Go back to that memory throughout the day as many times as you can.

Start Daydreaming

Imagine how you want your life to be. Start to create a new future for yourself in your mind, enjoy visiting how you will be, how you will act, how you will feel, how you will think. Maybe you want to lose weight. Imagine yourself your natural, desired shape. Maybe you want to be more confident. Daydream yourself acting confidently. Whatever daydream you choose, pay attention to daydreaming the thoughts and feelings you would have. Show your mind what you want and your mind will follow.

Strengths Gathering, Resilience Building

Reflect on past problem times you have lived through and reflect on how you managed to get through, reinforcing your capable side rather than criticising and worrying. At the same time you are valuing your gifts and talents that have supported you in life, building your self-belief.

List what happened:

- What did you do to overcome the problem/ difficulty?
- What thoughts and feelings helped you through?
- What thoughts and feelings made you feel less able?
- What help and resources did you access?
- What can you learn from this experience that was useful, your strengths and abilities to manage adversity?
- What will you do next time?

Be Your Best Friend

Imagine you are your best friend and list all the positive things a best friend, or anyone, has said to you or you would like them to say to you. Write these positive things down in your journal and reread the list throughout the day, week and months ahead while adding to it regularly as you become more attuned to creating and listening to the positive self-talk rather than criticism.

Watch Your Language

Be mindful of your thoughts and words—start listening to your words and thoughts—and whenever you find yourself experiencing a negative thought or saying something negative, imagine crossing it out in your mind and then think of something positive or say something positive. Use discernment: "it's not for me, I prefer..."

Exercise	**How did this go? Is this one you'll keep?**	**What did you learn about your thoughts, feelings and emotions? What's good for you? What's not so helpful?**
Day 1 Spin positive: inner critic triggers your best friend		
Day 2 Change routine		

Day 3 Happy memory		
Day 4 Daydreaming your future		
Day 5 Resilience building, strengths gathering		
Day 6 Be your best friend		
Day 7 Watch your language		

This chapter has mainly focused on exploring and auditing your self-belief and learning how to look after your self-belief, keeping it strong no matter where or what is happening in your life. This is an important aspect of your self-care and the first stage of Keeper

Habit Two. At the same time, you are getting into the routine of using Keeper Habit One. Using the Mb exercises to grow calm will also increase your self-awareness so that you can start connecting with the real you that works, acknowledging and valuing those parts of you that, if allowed, can trigger your natural confidence and ability to take control of your inner world. You can have full control over *you* when you know how.

Keeper Habits One and Two Combined

Keeper Habit One allows you to grow the space for Keeper Habit Two to take hold in your mind while constantly reducing your stress levels. Stress is normal, even helpful, but when we hold onto it and let it build, this is when the damage occurs. It brings you down and takes you apart. Using the Mb exercises you now have a mechanism to discharge stress and give you a chance to actually enjoy building you to enjoy the now.

Be kind to yourself. The fact you've got this book and are taking steps to change things is positive. It took you so many years to get here; allow the positive, boosting changes to happen gently and trust you are progressing, capable, able and deserving.

Inside, Outside and Outside

In this chapter you have discovered how to constantly nurture your self-belief and your confidence flow. It is important that we do not keep repairing and boosting gaps, but we use our new-found self-belief and confidence to meet our needs, and work to our strengths and talents. That is where our true contentment, success and happiness lies.

Case Study

A client came to see me after she had spent years looking after her ailing mother who now was in a nursing home. She found, despite this alleviating the pressure on her, she was becoming extremely stressed and anxious, worse than she had ever experienced. After doing the work of Keeper Habits One and Two she realised her strengths of caring and nurturing were important, but she had totally forgotten or did not know how to look after herself, her major asset! She had allowed others' needs to always be more important and now was the time to fill that gap in her knowledge and do the caring work for herself too. She resisted at first, which is usual, but very quickly she was able to rebuild her self-belief and confidence and make the most of her remaining time with her mother and start to explore living through her other strengths. Her progress was rapid and after just six weeks she reported "she felt a totally different person, happier and so much more relaxed".

Keeper Habit Three

Now you are feeling the benefits of Keeper Habits One and Two, you can use Keeper Habit Three to connect with yourself. Not the stressed, fearful or "should be" you but the real you that got buried underneath all of life's distractions. By distractions I mean all the responsibilities, all the criticisms that you keep using and hearing in a vain attempt to be successful, when in fact the opposite happens, more stress and more fear of failure and thinking you are not being good enough. Keeper Habit Three helps you get to know your strengths and talents and in turn how they can be developed to meet your needs and truly be you, successful you, knowing how to meet your needs and realising you have all the strengths and talents to meet your needs, wants and desires. You were born enough, we are all born enough, but somewhere along the way we start to question that, fail to access, grow and nurture our natural strengths and talents and the rest is exactly why you are reading this book. You suspected the truth... you are enough when you know how to support yourself in this modern world.

Key Takeaways

How to use Keeper Habit Two to repair and strengthen your self-belief:

- Build affirmations focused on building your self-belief because self-belief = self-esteem and self-confidence.
- Regularly check your self-belief for gaps and create affirmations to fill those gaps and strengthen yourself.
- Use a combination of Mb exercises (minimum six minutes a day) and affirmation repetitions to meet your needs for self-care.
- Aim for creating/repeating five affirmations: your five a day.
- Record your thoughts and feelings in your Success and Achievements Journal to program yourself for success.
- Create a feel-good anchor to maximise the good feelings in your day.
- Explore more ways to use journalling, noting down exercises that work well, goals, ideas and plans for the future.
- Keep using Keeper Habits One and Two and move on to Keeper Habit Three enjoying the benefits of Keeper Habits One and Two.

Further Reading

When the Body Says No: The Cost of Hidden Stress by Dr Gabor Maté, Vermilion

Feel the Fear...and Beyond: The Essential Companion to the Worldwide Bestseller Feel the Fear and Do It Anyway by Susan Jeffers

Teaching Clients to Use Mindfulness Skills: A Practical Guide by Christine Dunkley and Maggie Stanton

CHAPTER 4

Embrace Your Inner Compass: Living Authentically

Time to reconnect with your true self and make decisions that align with your deepest desires and values.

Keeper Habit Three: Keep the Real You as Your Life Guide to Your Strengths and Talents, Hopes and Dreams

Get to know the fearless, confident you, the real you that got buried under all that stress and anxiety. Explore and reclaim those unfulfilled desires and wishes that got squashed by your fear response, stress. Enjoy allowing them to blossom under the real safety mechanism we are all born with: our self-belief.

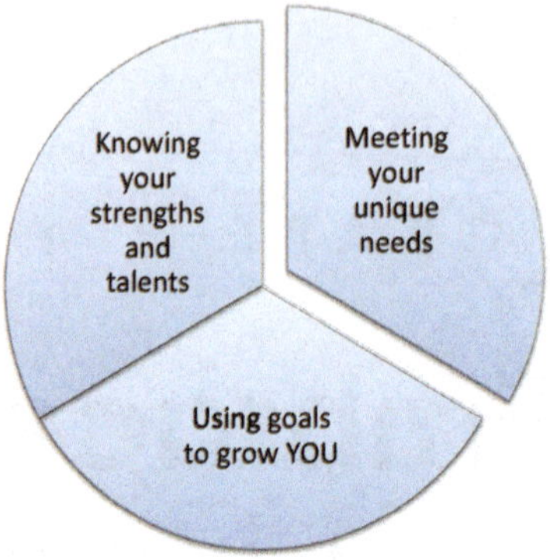

Going Forward from Your Beginning

As you work through this chapter, continue to write your answers in your journal. Focus on you, the real you, not the one that suits others' needs or expectations as you perceive them. Keeper Habit Three is all about getting to really know, love, accept and understand yourself. Accepting yourself "warts and all" knowing you are good enough. Allowing yourself to pick and choose how and what you want more of, freeing *you* to show up in everything you do, hope to be and do. That hoping and wishing is a part of who you are at this moment and, if you choose, could be the small shoots of what you want to grow more of, to shape the world you live in. This is not about changing yourself into the person someone else wants you to be. This is about finding out and really loving you, whatever or wherever you are now, in this moment and looking forward, with confidence and trust in life.

Not Sure What Your Needs Are? Your Purpose in Life?

This exercise is developed on Martin Seligman's positive psychology system to identify our real needs. Knowing the real you better equips you to maintain your unique blend of well-being. For each of us our needs are different but how to look after yourself is the same and doable. When you understand your needs, you can meet them in your inner and outer world with ease. Your needs are where your unique talents and strengths lie, specifically designed for you to grow your talents and strengths to equip you to easily meet your needs.

You Have All You Need

It makes sense. Where we have needs, we also have the beginnings of the necessary talents and strengths. Our life purpose is to use and develop our unique combination of talents and strengths and thrive. If we do not understand our own needs, we cannot fully access our talents and strengths, and those strengths and talents become weaker or even fail to materialise. This gap in who we are meant to be can leave us prey to a range of unhelpful feelings such as dissatisfaction, stress, low mood and other moods and unable to understand why. Frequently we then look outside ourselves for comfort, maybe food, alcohol, unhealthy relationships or strive to fit in being something or someone we were never meant to be.

Exercise: Needs, Talents and Strength Finder Exercise

The Needs, Talents and Strength Finder exercise is an opportunity to take some time to explore your strengths and your natural abilities. You can then audit how much you are allowing your natural talents and strengths to show up in your everyday life. Take the time to think about each statement. I really suggest you do the exercise over a few days rather than in one sitting. The exercise is long, but you are important and definitely worth it. Reflect on each strength and remember times when you used these strengths or even times when you wanted to, how you felt, what you thought and what it made you wish for you, feel, want for you. It is important to note that it is not necessarily how strong or evident these talents or strengths are in your life at the moment. It is about how they feel and attract you when they occur.

Score Yourself out of 10 for Each Statement

Watch out for any little judgemental or critical voices that may come up. Those thoughts that may have made you withdraw from any of these strengths. Just ignore them or replace them with a growth thought such as "I deserve this, I am good enough, I want to shine as me". Deal with what you truly feel, want and think, not what you think you should be feeling, wanting and thinking.

Be confident in your own interpretation of the strength or talent as you are illuminating your strengths and talents, so your understanding and the score out of 10 you choose for each statement will be perfect for you.

1. Achiever: wanting to achieve something, finish it or working towards a goal.
2. Action focus: a need to get on, take action, get started and carry on.
3. Adaptability: a flexible approach to things, getting lost in time, able to live in the moment.
4. Analytical: you like to view the evidence and proof in order to accept something as true for you.
5. Arranger: you like to organise and arrange things.
6. Beliefs: you have clear beliefs that need to be met for you in many/most situations before you can engage.

7. Leader: you are comfortable leading and naturally take command.
8. Communication: you enjoy and need to communicate with others.
9. Competitive: you like to compete and enjoy winning and/or being in the top few, out in front, ahead.
10. Connecting: you value others as much as yourself and you enjoy companionship.
11. Context: you understand things better when the context is clear or based on your experience.
12. Scrutiniser: you identify and assess risks naturally and automatically.
13. Developer: you like helping others to achieve their potential. You find it easy to believe in others' potential.
14. Discipline: you enjoy an organised, controlled and planned world. Surprises or unexpected events that interrupt your world are never or rarely welcome, e.g. something stops working, a last-minute invitation, unexpected/invited visitors, etc.
15. Empathy: you notice and pick up on others' emotions easily.

16. Fairness: equality and balance are extremely important to you.
17. Focus: you find it easy and natural to prioritise your goals and to focus on a goal.
18. Futuristic: the future intrigues you and you are very forward-thinking.
19. Harmony: you enjoy agreement, conflict is something you avoid and you work hard to achieve balance and harmony in all your connections.
20. Ideas-led: you enjoy and have lots of ideas, some good and some not so good.
21. Inclusive: you enjoy including people, bringing everyone together to feel a part of something important.
22. One-on-one focus: you enjoy people as individuals and have a diverse range of friends from varying backgrounds, beliefs, social groups, ages, etc. preferring smaller or one-to-one interactions.
23. Learning new information: you enjoy learning about things and new information, ideas and concepts capture your attention.
24. Thinking: mental activity and thinking about things is important to you and is something you naturally do.

25. Learner: you enjoy taking a course, learning about something new and/or in more depth, exploring topics that interest you through further study. You enjoy formal and informal research and learning methods.
26. Best focus: you strive for excellence, not perfection, but the very best in things, the optimal level you can achieve with the time and resources available to you.
27. Positive focus: you naturally look for the good, positive things in people, events, situations, etc. Everything has a good side to it.
28. Friendship-based: you enjoy and feel most comfortable being with friends and like-minded people.
29. Responsible approach: you easily take on responsibility and enjoy your role to solve issues/problems.
30. Bringing things into order: you enjoy and gain satisfaction from solving problems, puzzles, quizzes, etc.
31. Self-confidence in your own strengths and abilities: you naturally believe, most times, in yourself, your abilities and capabilities.
32. Significant: you need to feel you matter to others in particular. You are most secure

when you feel important to and considered by others.

33. Strategic in approach: you enjoy finding the best way for the best results and answers. You are able to imagine consequences and adjustments to get the best results.
34. Persuasiveness: you can easily win others over to your way of thinking and doing things.
35. Add any others that you see as your strength, such as humour, warm-heartedness, amenability, ability to work alone, enjoy solitude, etc. All these can fit into the others, but it is important you recognise them to add value to this exercise. Add them onto your list now with a score. The more you focus and think about you, who you are, the more that will help you value yourself and know who you are, not what others expect you to be or who you think others expect you to be or who you think you should be.

Moving On to the Next Stage in This Exercise

Go back over your list and under the highest scoring strengths write down how this is showing up in your life. For example, for me, it is communicator. This shows up in my world through writing books and delivering training courses. Another, for me, is learning and achieving. I always have a course I am planning to attend or actually attending; sometimes it is for a hobby, sometimes it is professional. It is my thing, what I do, learn and grow.

My needs	How that shows up in my life	How much does it feature in daily or weekly life? Do you want more or less or the same?
Communicator	Writing, training, friends, volunteering (formal and informal)	Formal: 30 per cent, feels okay Informal: 20 per cent, feels okay

The Final Stage

Review your answers and start to look at the strengths you would enjoy having a chance to show up more in your daily life. Moving forward in your life, remember your needs, strengths and talents and let them be your guide when making decisions on what is right for you. It may be useful to make a list now of those needs, talents and strengths and make a note against those you want to bring in, strengthen and expand in your life. This helps to program your mind to choosing and attracting the right opportunities for you when they emerge into your world, your daily life. Understanding your talents and strengths can also encourage you to do things in your daily life or workplace in a way that enables you to use and develop your strengths and talents. Use this list as a handy reminder for you of those opportunities (however scary) you need to include to meet your needs to support your happiness, contentment and well-being.

Your Life Purpose

This is simple to find now; just choose opportunities, work, hobbies and leisure which allow you to develop, grow and realise your strengths and talents. Your purpose is to meet your needs by using, developing and growing your unique set of talents and strengths.

Own Your Paybacks

Most of us have to do things we do not, or think we do not, enjoy and that may be because we have decided they are not enjoyable and therefore insist on not doing them, not enjoying them and even struggling to do them. Now I ask you to find ways to use your strengths and talents while doing them. Turn those tasks, duties or whatever into opportunities to be you, really you. When we do things with resentment, wishing we did not have to, we are only feeding our ego, not our true identity, needs or ability to have a stress-free time. Say, for example, you hate cleaning the bathroom. Instead, you just make your payback hate and set up the inner dialogue, thoughts, emotions and actions to prove you're right. Being right only feeds the ego beyond your identity, not your need to use and develop your strengths and talents. The next time you find yourself with a "chore" either paid, or seemingly unpaid, decide to bring in a "payback" that meets your needs. Use the "chore" to do an Mb exercise or "act as if" this was the most important thing to do and totally focus on the task. Notice the touch and smell sensations, another type of meditation, thus feeding your mind and natural capacity for peace, making room for you to strengthen and grow.

Add In Your Values

This is the context you like to meet your needs through your talents and strengths. To help you decide what is truly important to you, your true values, not others' values or what others may think, get familiar with your values. Values make us tick, they lead us to our purpose, our fulfilled life. They are never right or wrong; they are simply what matters to us, makes us unique and makes our life work for us.

What Do You Value?

Knowing your values helps you move away from your shoulds, coulds, past conditioning, would haves and if onlys to really look at and get to know what you truly value, what is important to you, just you. In this wonderful world of choice there are lots of things you could get involved in and lots of things that are begging for your attention. Rather than add to your life they can just distract and confuse you, thus raising the stress levels. It makes sense to check out what is important to you, your values. Simply put, it is a back-to-basics approach. Your needs, strengths and talents need to shine on/in the things, context, that matter to you.

Same Needs, Different Values

I love coaching, writing and training to help people. I could do this just as well with cosmetic surgery or make-up but for me it is all about the inner world, who you are, not what you look like. I leave that to others. For someone else it may be helping people to make the very best of their appearance and so they write, coach and train people and love their work. Same strengths and talents, different context, different values. Not right or wrong, just different!

Exercise: Must Have Pyramid: Finding Your Values

What to Do

Get together 10 pieces of paper, big enough to write one word on each. I find Post-its work brilliantly for this exercise, as it stops the 10 pieces of paper getting lost, wandering, etc.

1. Clear your mind using three even breaths. https://fionachapmanspodcast.buzzsprout.com/1882592/9531133
2. Now ask yourself "what's important to me?" Only accept one-word answers. One-word answers are important. As soon as you start putting your answers into sentences you'll start justifying, explaining and the conscious mind will start changing things. Allow the first thing that comes into your mind to be your answer. Accept it and write it down.
3. Write down your one-word answers on your pieces of paper. One word per piece of paper until you have a word on each of your 10 pieces of paper. Remember, no repeats.
4. If you have a repeat answer, that's fine. Just ask yourself the question again: "what's important to me" until you get something new. If you get stuck use the "Soothing Breath" exercise to help you to relax and focus!

   https://fionachapmanspodcast.buzzsprout.com/1882592/9531186

5. Now arrange your pieces of paper into a pyramid. Put the most important words at the top and the less important at the bottom of your pyramid. Using Post-its helps as you can stick them to a large sheet of paper to look at. Note they are all important; you are deciding the ranking of importance in this exercise.

The important thing is to go for one-word answers, no sentences, and no judgements on what comes up!

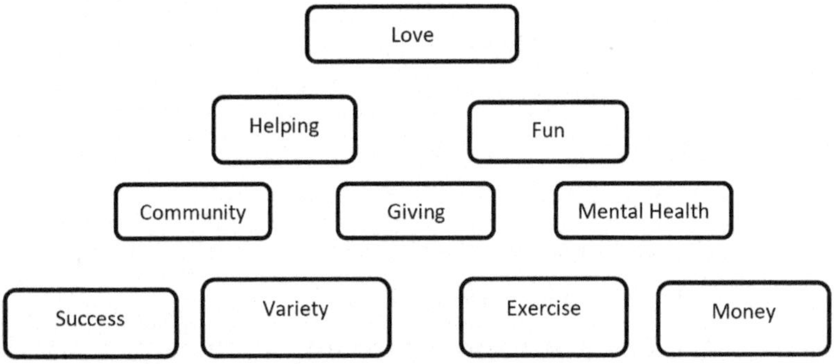

Most Important Versus Less Important and All Are Important

Ranking (by sorting your "must haves" into a pyramid shape) is a vital part of this process. Ranking shows you your most important words in terms of percentage; however, for a balanced life you need *all* aspects showing up. Ranking helps you realise the amount they matter to you in relation to each other. For example, money ranks at the bottom for me, but it is still important, critical, as it enables and frees me to be active in all the other things. Do not forget any one of your "must haves", just start to be aware of how they each contribute to a lifestyle that works for you.

Case Study

A client told me she loved her job and she didn't mind working long hours. However, she was starting to feel her job was taking over her life now. There was no time for anything else, any of the other essential things for her. Rather than blame her job she was able to work out what she needed and look for similar work that allowed her enough time to meet all her needs. In fact, she discussed the problem with her boss and got her hours changed. The money was less (though she still could meet all her commitments) but it mattered more that she had time for one of her passions, painting, as in decorating houses! I believe half the problem of getting what you need is really knowing all your needs and how much of each you need! Incidentally, she has totally tipped the balance; three years later she has her own decorating business and volunteers in the place she used to work. Another important point is to remember our capacity to grow, what suits us now, may not suit us as well in a few years' time.

Explore Now Using Your Values Matched to Your Life as It Is Now

Try this in different situations and parts of your life: your roles, daily work, relationships, etc. This is not to say anything is right or wrong, but this helps you shape your life to not only use and develop your strengths and talents but also in the right context for you, the things you value.

As you travel through life and reach different phases of your life and develop, your values and needs *may* change. That's fine and worth remembering. I like to do a check as part of setting my intentions (where I am going) for the New Year and see what is important to me now. I always set a few goals but focus on my intentions to work towards something, being open to opportunities that may arise along the way. Just consider and decide on your goals and intentions, check them against your "must haves" and then enjoy the journey. Focusing just on the goal can be inflexible and indicate an end rather than a flow and progress in life which, I believe, is more realistic. This way we are clear about our direction, our essential intentions, and saying no becomes more about saying yes to you, your decisions and your intentions. Ask yourself when opportunities and requests arise if this takes me closer to my intentions and my essential values, talents and strengths, which then becomes a direct action to support you, your growth and development.

Back to the Now: Your Current Life/Lifestyle

- How do you use your roles in life to express your needs, talents and strengths? Are you allowing your values to shine through your current life roles? (By needs I mean your opportunity to grow and use your talents and strengths. Needs come from within us, and it is our responsibility to meet our own needs.)
- How do your other activities help you enjoy and create a life that you feel you are living according to your values and choosing opportunities to use and grow your natural talents and strengths?
- Or have stress and others' demands (or so you think) taken over?

Gently Reshape Your Life to Suit You

Now you are working with who you are, what suits you, your needs and your natural talents and strengths, make a list of your top seven (needs) talents and strengths and keep your value pyramid to hand.

The next exercise helps you check how and if you are fully expressing the important stuff in you and your life and notice opportunities for more or less or a mindset that would suit you better and help you grow, not your ego distorting and hiding your needs.

Getting Started

Do both exercises—the Must Have Pyramid and the My Roles exercises—to help you find where you are able to express those things that are essential to you, your needs, talents and strengths and values. In short, it may be a recognised role; for example, mother, son or daughter is an opportunity to be those important things that make up the uniqueness of you. If you recognise what you need and balance those needs, you are on a pathway to feeling more "you" in your life. Now is the time to stop trying and enjoy just being you.

How are you bringing and expressing your natural strengths, potential and values in your life?

Case Study

Here is an example from a client who just felt something was missing. She stated she didn't want to change anything and felt she had a good life and should be more grateful! Her essential values were family, loving, friends, creative, respect, talents, alone, independence, learning and security.

My roles	My values and potential talents and strengths I am able to express in this role	Percentage of my current life activities
Mother	family, loving, nurturing	
Artist	friends, creative, respect, talents, alone, independence, learning, security	
Friend	family, loving, friends, creative, respect, talents, independence, learning, security	

Now It's Your Turn

Put all of your roles in the list and enjoy finding out how and if they give you an opportunity to express your values, strengths and talents, those things important for you to have and be in your life. Make the list as long or as short as you like, add to it gradually, or if you prefer, avoid the hierarchy of a list and just make a bubble gram (see example) to get started. This is you getting to know you, focus inwards to understand and meet your needs, rather than outwards. Your life becomes your opportunity to enjoy meeting your needs within your values rather than being persuaded by external factors that have no links to you decide what suits you best, what you need. The world, your outer world, has everything you need, you just need to understand, learn what you need and learn to use your inner world to reflect your outer world.

My roles	**My values and potential talents and strengths I am able to express in this role**	**Percentage of my current life activities/time**
Being Me		

Bubble gram example

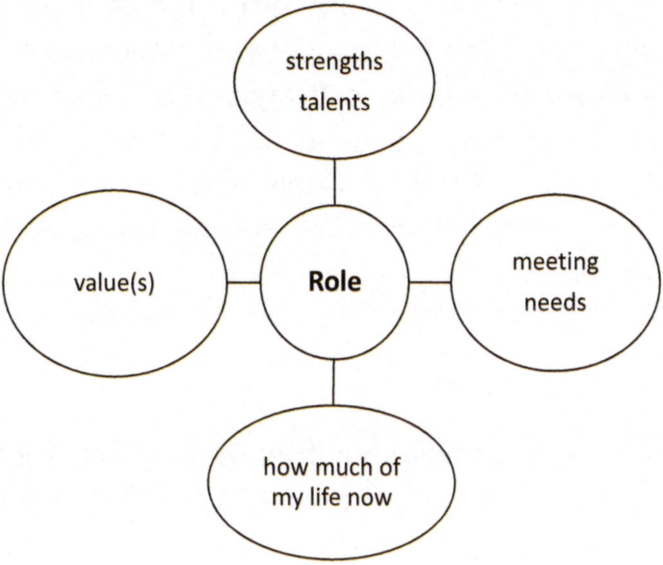

Nourish Your Needs and Values

Are there any gaps? Are there things missing? Is the balance right? Check against your record of values and needs to use your strengths and talents. Maybe the amounts showing up need rebalancing to suit you, maybe things can go, maybe you need to exercise your talents and strengths more. Your potential is infinite. More of this and less of that? Now stress becomes your early alert system to access your talents and strengths, work within your values, be you rather than what you have misguidedly learnt you "should be". Ignore your stress early warning signal and the stress just keeps building.

Purpose in Life

Your purpose in life is to use, grow and develop your strengths and talents that meet your needs. So rather that look for something to "fix you", just look for how you can meet your needs in the outside world and your inner world too. You only have to "be you" to find your purpose, no more looking for something you must do.

Stress as a Life Ally

Stress now becomes your friend, an early warning system that you are not looking after you, allowing you to be enough, not healing the gap and instead allowing the stress in rather than your natural confidence to flow. Remember stress is there to give us a boost, an alert to action, focus and then we discharge the stress when we have responded appropriately.

Case Study

One of my clients was feeling very bogged down with the caring responsibilities for two elderly members of her family, one was in a care home and the other in their own home. Both needed support in different ways and my client was finding it was taking over her life. With a full-time job and teenage family it seemed that everything was just too much. After we looked at her values, talents and strengths it was clear caring was a big part of who she was, but she also had other needs and values leaving little or no room for all her needs, making her feel constantly overwhelmed. It doesn't have to be a big change; it can just be something small to start that change. For example, if you find you don't have enough fun in your life, do something to bring in fun. Watch a funny show on TV, go to the mirror and pull a funny face, start making room for fun every day in your life. Whatever you focus on you get more of. Fact. Make a list of quick fun things you can do for just a few minutes. Her list included things like looking at a funny family photo, watching a comedy on television, ten minutes enjoying a cup of tea.

She started just looking for fun and whenever she felt the stress rising, she did a Mb exercise and did something from the fun list she had compiled. Sometimes she could not do her fun thing straight away, so instead she planned when she could do it on that day, and put it in her calendar. Just that focus on fun was a step towards changing and getting out of her "critical head".

Set a goal now to bring in the fun; fun lightens the mood, clears the way for you to clearly see how you need to live, so it is a really good starting point and pays back quickly. Start small and see how it feels, then gently grow it.

Keeper Habit Three into Goal Setting with Intention

Now you are beginning to understand how to commit to being you and allowing the gaps to heal, it is likely that you want to make some changes. Maybe how you go about life and set some reminders/intentions/ goals to bring in the things you want, enabling your unique set of needs, talents, strengths and values to shine. Deciding on what you want to grow to meet your needs is critical for you—fail to plan, plan to fail. If you do not know where you are going, what "successful" life you wish to create, then you can just make your intentions to use the keeper habits and gradually your answers will emerge.

Key Takeaways

How to use Keeper Habit Three to reconnect with your true self and meet your unique needs:

- Explore your strengths and natural abilities using the Needs, Talents and Strength Finder exercise.

- Find your values with the Must Have Pyramid exercise and explore how these relate to your life.
- Use the My Roles exercise combined with the Must Have Pyramid to help you identify what you need to activate your values, strengths and talents.
- Use Keeper Habit Three to transform your needs into goal setting.

Further Reading

Authentic Happiness: Using the New Positive Psychology by Martin Seligman

How To Get What You Want: And Want What You Have by John Gray

Loving What Is by Byron Katie with Stephen Mitchell

The Rainbow Factor: 7 Steps to Life Engagement by Frances Tolton

CHAPTER 5

The Breakthrough: Turning Transformation into Manifestation

You can unleash your inner power to create real, tangible success and live the life you've envisioned or maybe even resigned to fantasy. You can and you will; now and your future nows are yours to create, enjoy and succeed!

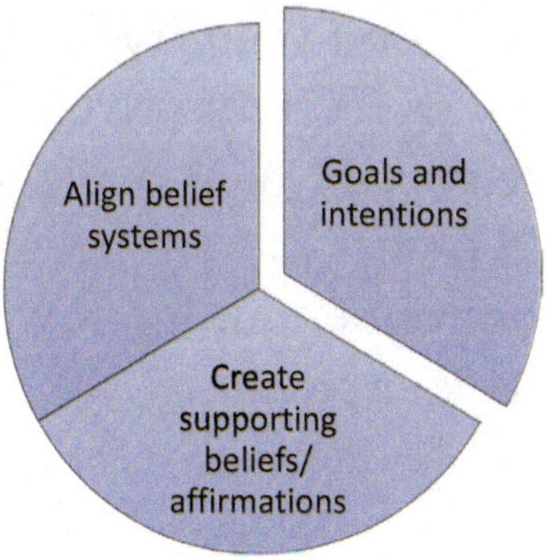

Start Getting What You Want

Now you have mastered your stress habit and rebuilt your self-belief, keep growing. Recognise and use your power to transform, reshape and create, and enjoy the success you deserve. Allow you to shine through and be supported by your true strengths and talents to live your most successful, comfortable, stress-free life.

That's Life

Challenges can be chosen and just happen regardless of what we ordered or want; some good, some not so comfortable, "it just is". If there is a struggle, a block, get used to strengthening yourself. Read struggles and blockages as a trigger to adjust and strengthen you to handle those challenges and goals in the manner you desire. When life brings along something we did not "order" we can use those very skills to get us through the tougher, more challenging times with more ease. Much better to learn the skills when the going is good than trying to work on our inner world when we feel ourselves struggling; but, no matter, what you do to support yourself is the same in all good times. You are never helpless. You are always in control of your inner world when you know how to use your power.

Aiming for Wants and Improvements in Your Life

It is the nature of humankind to want more, and, as we become stronger and free of the stress burden, it is likely your increased energy and zest for life will encourage you to want more for you. Long-buried desires and dreams may now start to surface and now you can choose for you.

Stress-Free, Not Challenge Free

There will always be stress but now, using the keeper habits, you can use stress to support you, to be brave, take the right action for you, to create the life that suits you and quickly release any stress. The keeper habits are constantly increasing your self-awareness, your ability to tune into you and keep on growing, building your resilience and thriving—no longer just coping or worse! You are free to do whatever you need to do, want to do and "empty your stress bucket" regularly, habitually, so you can play, relax and enjoy being you. You are enough and always have been!

Choice, Not Stress

You have achieved your first goal using the keeper habits to master your stress habit and build yourself up. So what will you choose for yourself now? You have a choice. It was the gap in your knowledge that tricked you into thinking stress was the only option for you. Now you know better, you can have and deserve more when you want more.

Self-Belief = Self-Esteem + Confidence

Build upon your strengthened self-belief and continue the focus on you and what you want to create and bring into your life. Now you can choose goals and challenges beyond being free of the stress burden. Choose whatever successful living means for you and that may mean just enjoying your life as it is now.

Matching Your Beliefs to Your Goals

However, if you choose to create goals to start living the life you choose, to suit you, it is easy once you know the rules to guide you. Big or small goals and intentions, it is important to be clear about what you want to achieve and steer your daily intentions to achieving. Once you are really clear about what you want you can start work on your inner world to accelerate your progress.

Goals Which Generate Intentions

First you decide your goals, what you want for you in your life, and then you choose and check your beliefs, including self-beliefs, to help you make those changes. All of these actions demand change in us and as change is unchartered territory it can appear hard, difficult, tempting to withdraw to a place of safety no matter how much we desire the change. It helps if we consider change as a process. Often, we expect change to be an immediate thing and then berate ourselves just as we start to enter the change process and give up before we transition to the new.

Timing Is Important

What we focus on is what we get and part of the law of attraction's role in reaching our goals is all about the timing. Sometimes we have control over the when, sometimes we need to allow things to unfold when the time is right. Our external goals frequently require things that are beyond our control to be in place. This is where the trust part of the law of attraction comes into being. It really does help to get clear about your areas of control and influence and stick firmly within them. If you find you are losing faith in your goals, getting impatient, then it is definitely an internal goal that needs setting to support your progress, and you have total control over that!

Living with Intentions

Nowadays we often expect things to be immediate, and if not, we can start to trigger stress as our response.

When we focus on daily, achievable intentions it helps the power of attraction to allow the timing factor to be perfect for us and also keeps us feeling, believing, we are making progress, which we are, of course. How many times in your life have you experienced a disappointment or a setback and what happened next turned that disappointment into a "good job that happened" situation? Intentions help you to trust, do your bit for things to happen and enjoy the journey, all the time creating and doing things with intention. Allowing for living in the now.

Internal Goals to Support You

A client decided she wanted to increase her earnings by 100 per cent in the field she worked in = external goal.

Internal goals = strengthen confidence and self-esteem, strengthen beliefs in deserving abundance/ money, its flow and constant availability.

Finding and Creating the Goals to Suit the Unique You

Choose a fresh page in your journal and head it "Goals and Intentions". (If you are using the *Mind Your Gap* journal there is a page already set up for your goals and intentions.) First, jot down your goals: the things you want to bring into your life.

Edit your goals to follow the absolutes of goal setting.

Your goals, desires, are designed to:

- Meet your needs and allow you to grow your strengths and talents.
- Focus on your areas of control and influence.
- Totally achieve what you want; no one else, no shoulds, coulds or oughts.
- Be stated in the positive—only include what you want. Remember "reverse brainstorming" (state what you do not want, then state what you do want) can help you find what you do want if you find yourself stuck in what you do not want.

Check Your "Must Haves" and Values

Make sure you check you are meeting your values, one, some or all. Notice the proportion of your values met by your goals. Does it leave room in your life for any other values and needs to be met? Do they balance your needs, meeting what is important to you at this time in your life? You may wish to do the exercise again and again as you read through this book. Do not be shy of making changes to suit you. Your needs will change internally and externally as your understanding of yourself and your needs grows and emerges. Do not forget to allow those changes to develop by recognising they are a change and change is a process, not a full stop. The external stuff is great too. All those modern-day trappings and developments are to be selected, aspired to and enjoyed to suit you. However, it's knowing you are suiting you, not responding to some clever marketing or your ego getting out of control. So be playful, see, feel and pick your top five priorities as you travel through this book and your life.

Have a Look at Some Sample Goals. This Is How You Decide to Change

Decision to change generates a goal: I look after my body by exercising and keeping fit. New fitness regimen.

> Decision/goal: I complete all my tasks/reports effortlessly and on time. I now say yes to what is important and have enough time to do everything. In conflict of time and priority situations I will negotiate and agree priorities with my boss/business partner.

> Decision/goal: I have a wonderful partner who meets all my needs. I look for ways to nurture our relationship that takes both our needs into account. If I am not happy, I talk about it.

Decision/goal: My services are in great demand; I have many paying customers. I write a marketing plan and regularly follow through according to the plan. I continue to develop my skills through professional CPD and training.

Decision/goal: I maintain a healthy weight. I choose healthy foods that support my natural body shape and health.

Decision/goal: I easily meet my sales targets. I focus on developing and increasing the number of relationships with clients and keep up to date with new products and share them regularly with my clients.

For each goal, start to develop and examine their strength, their alignment with you, for you and the actions. Daily intentions become your focus to achieve the goal.

Manifesting Your Goal Exercise

Write as much as you can so you really understand what you want, the impact of the changes on you, your life and any potential impact on those important things or people in your life.

When I am… or When I have… or When… (*I have achieved my goal)*

1. I am ____________________
2. It is important to me because ____________________
3. It is right for me because ____________________
4. My goal allows me to ____________________
5. I am able to ____________________
6. I (do/learn/develop/grow) ____________________
7. I am easily being ____________________
8. I feel (describe those emotions in detail) ____________________
9. My days are
   I am
   My surroundings are ____________________
10. How this affects those that are important to me? (If it matters to you what others will think, do, then ask them! Don't expect to know what others will think, do, feel!) ____________________
11. How do I know these things are right for me? ____________________

You may not have all the answers but by asking the question you will start the process of having your goal, deciding its importance and the benefits it will bring for you and your world.

Mind-Reading, Not a Success

If your goal will impact on others who are important to you, then it is critical to find out how they would react, get them on board, find out if they agree and to check that you are okay with any consequences you may perceive possible at this stage. Remember, you are not a fortune-teller or mind-reader! If you have someone important in your life, do not presume to know how they would react when you change or achieve, what they would do or what they would think.

Alternatively, you would, of course, only check out with others who you are keen to keep in your life. That does not mean they will have a casting vote. I am just saying you need to fully explore the impact of a goal. Some goals have no impact while others are big and alongside the exploration process you will also find your supporters and cheerleaders.

Decided Your Goal or Goals?

Now make sure you understand your area of control within the goal you have chosen. Check your understanding is aligned with the real areas of control you have, and the influence you have, and the control and influence you do not have.

Control and Influence

It is really important that our goals, and then intentions, support what is within our control. Say, for example, you decide you want to be a millionaire in five years. Yes, all this is possible but just saying it over and over again and imagining being a millionaire is not going to make it happen. You know in reality money comes through work, business acumen, good investments or maybe inheritance. Which do you have control over? It makes sense you have the biggest control over earning money through work or business in some form. You can influence a financial reward by investments through knowledge, calculating and selecting the appropriate risk level, knowing about the markets. However, you do not have control over many variables on the market. Maybe you will work out how much you need to earn over the next "how many years" and then take steps to make that happen. You have your goal, and you then have your intentions to earn so much at each stage, save so much and every opportunity that comes your way you will be able to judge its relevance to you and your goal.

Control and Influence: Test Your Goal and Your Intentions

Focusing on what is out of our control, or even influence, is how we build our stress. Maybe you are at risk or perceive yourself to be at risk of being made redundant. The resultant worry and stress will depend very much on if you focus on your areas of control and influence or focus continually on things you do not have control over or any real influence. Use the diagram below and check your goal and intentions are focusing in your areas of control and influence.

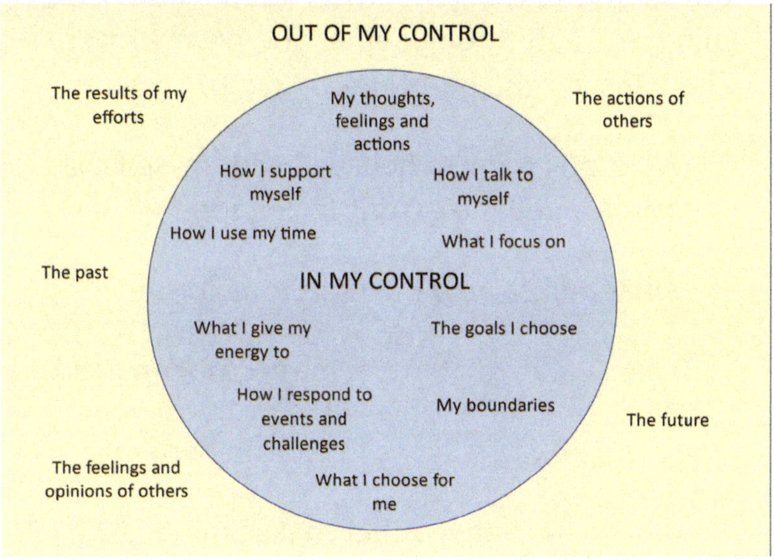

For example, maybe your child throws a tantrum in the morning, making everyone late. What you do have total control over is how you respond and allow and plan time for this possibility or event. If the time is not needed just relax together, talk and listen; better than both of you being upset.

Success and Achievements Journal: Allow the Truth out Exercise

Write out the statement

"I have not reached/tried for my goal before because..."

Just allow yourself to keep answering the question above. Keep writing and after ten minutes, read through what you have written. Then answer the questions below:

What do I think or believe about myself that has stopped me getting/going for my goal?

What makes now the right time for me?

When is the right time for me to go for my goal?

What are my reasons for starting now?

What has changed that makes me believe I could achieve this goal now?

What needs to change to make my goal possible now?

Use this review and reflect process to check you know exactly what you want, and it suits you enough for now. Keep adding to and changing your goal until you decide it is detailed enough, clear to you and absolutely right for you now. If you find yourself shrinking your goal, just recognise it is fear and fear is an illusion to keep you safe; you can always build in steps and smaller goals to your bigger goal.

Spotting the Barriers We Create

Now is the time to decide what beliefs will help you achieve your goal. Remember to bring in those beliefs and allow unhelpful beliefs to fade away. What you focus on becomes more real, reflecting and bringing it into your world, your reality.

Your Goal as a Clear Direction

Once you have decided on your goal, write it out SMARTLY.

Specific

Measurable

Achievable

Realistic

Timebound

Loving You

About specific. If it's too vague, it is always unreachable. I want to be successful in my career, I want to be a perfect mother, I want to spend more time on hobbies—all far too vague. Specific examples: I want to reach 20,000 sales by April 2023, I want to be able to count to 10 before responding to the children at the end of the day, I want to spend three hours each week on crafting/ running/ whatever your chosen hobby is for you. Knowing exactly what you want you can start creating your intentions, the daily steps to making it happen. If a goal feels a burden, then break it down into smaller chunks and start working with the smallest chunk.

Here are some extra tips to help you attract your goal into your life and experience your goal happening in your life *now* with your daily intentions supporting your regular, consistent progress.

Use the Goal Worksheet at the End of This Chapter

Use the 3D Directed Daydreaming Technique

Help your goal take root and create your daily intentions. Whenever you have a moment, allow your mind to wander and daydream what it will be like having your goal. Let your mind enjoy every moment while you daydream what it is like to have your goal. Experience, through daydreaming, having totally reached your goal and living with it in place, achieved.

Notice how your body feels, listen to the thoughts you have, the feelings and emotions you experience having your goal. The daydreaming activity helps to create a can-do mindset and a belief that you can and will really complete/achieve your goal, an inner knowing leading to increased motivation and focus. Jot down these findings in your journal, as those are the feelings/beliefs you can grow through your daily exercises by including them in your affirmations and intentions.

Mirror Work

Every morning when you are getting yourself ready for your day, make sure you take a few moments and look deeply into your eyes in the mirror and repeat your goal(s). Best to repeat three times to allow the knowledge to sink into your subconscious and support you to complete your daily intention(s). You may feel a bit odd doing this but remember the subconscious is very black and white and believes what it is told. If you believe it, you can create it. This exercise helps you strengthen your self-belief that your goal is for you, and it is just a matter of time before you achieve it.

Make a To-Do List—Support Your Mind to Engage

Every night, build your intentions into your actions for tomorrow. The nightly "to-do list" made just before you go to sleep helps to program your mind ready to complete the tasks. Remember that your to-do list needs to be achievable with something that can be done or begun tomorrow.

Write or Word-Process

Use your journal to write out your goal(s) and intention(s) on a daily basis. This helps keep them firmly in your consciousness and pushed onwards towards your long-term memory, your subconscious. Regularly writing down your goal(s) and the following day's intentions allows you to see opportunities and options as they occur, thus speeding up your progress.

Maybe you have heard the urban myth about the Harvard or Yale University students who wrote down their goals and were more successful than those who did not write down their goals. Well, that study did happen, but it was conducted by Gail Matthews, PhD, at Dominican University with 149 students. There is proof that goals or intentions benefit from being written down and success increases still more if you also include a friend as a supporter, someone to share progress with regularly.

Use the Mb exercises from Keeper Habit One to grow into enjoying where you are now, as part of your journey

You've Gotta Be Here to Go There!

Regularly tap into your inner wisdom and discuss your intentions with your older self. Use the "Talking to Your Older Self" exercise (https://soundcloud.com/user-135417655/talking-to-your-older-self-from-how-to-mind-your-gap-betweem-stress-and-success-book-1-release-date-april-2025?si=b1391de3420b4c85b6d4b6e4744d35d7&utm_source=clipboard&utm_medium=text&utm_campaign=social_sharing) as an opportunity to explore, gain support, report progress, problem solve and tap into your inner guidance and wisdom. This journey with your older self really helps you to tune in with you and your inner knowing, your intuition. The full exercise can be found at the end of the chapter.

Grow Your Personal Power

No matter what your goal is, if you do not believe, deep down, you deserve it you will always scupper your success. Our beliefs are our drivers; use your affirmations to boost your beliefs that your goal is for you, and you deserve to be successful, now and always. Affirmations by their nature, and repetition, help us learn new things, new beliefs, that support our goal achievement.

Case Study

Another client I worked with stated she had always struggled with low self-esteem and confidence, and this was likely to have shaped her career choices. She spent years working in the service industry, alternating between reception and table waiting, roles she mostly enjoyed because of the people contact. Boredom with her work began to weigh heavily on her, leading to increasing feelings of frustration, low mood and a belief that she had little to offer beyond the confines of these jobs.

At a particularly low point, my client decided she needed a change and began sessions with me. She began exploring her feelings and the gaps between her current situation and the life she envisioned. She had long ago stopped tapping into her imagination, creating dreams and hopes for herself.

The 3D Directed Daydreaming exercise helped her reconnect with her long-forgotten dreams and hopes of being a nurse, opening her mind to the possibilities. Through self-reflection, self-belief and strengths and gifts assessments this client uncovered a long-standing interest in healthcare—a field she had never pursued since long ago she was told her maths was not good enough. This was from a so-called friend in her teens, but had obviously stuck and shaped her future choices.

Alongside building her self-belief and developing her strengths and gifts she began volunteering at a local hospital. Though hesitant at first, she quickly realised that she loved helping others and found fulfilment in the environment. Encouraged by this experience, she applied for a position as a nursing assistant, a role that gave her hands-on experience and a deeper understanding of patient care.

The experience reignited her passion for learning and gave her the confidence to pursue further education. This client then took a maths course and then successfully enrolled in physiotherapy training, a path she once thought unattainable. Today, she is thriving in her studies, excelling in clinical placements, and envisioning a future where she can make a meaningful difference in patients' lives.

I share this client's journey to show how self-awareness (Keeper Habit One) can lead to the ability to fill those gaps in our self-belief (Keeper Habit Two) and discover and use our natural strengths and gifts to build our authentic life, one that is chosen by us, our hopes and desires for ourselves. Identify, remove barriers to your goal.

Sometimes patterns, old learning and ways of thinking will not work in our now and, in fact, cause the very problems and blockages we are trying to resolve by aiming for a goal. The situation you are in now is something that you believed, on some level, often unconsciously, you deserved. That is all well and good if the situation suits you but if you have decided to aim for something more, different, better, it is important you work on your beliefs as much as your steps to achieving the goal.

Be brave and act "as if" you have already achieved your goal. Get familiar and used to enjoying the thoughts, feelings, emotions and actions having your goal will bring about. If you are aiming for abundance this does not mean actually having the outward aspects of abundance but focusing on the inner experience of abundance. Paying bills with an easy mindset, feeling relaxed about money, living within your current level of abundance with ease, enjoying looking forward to acquiring material things when the time is right, opening a savings account and saving, even if it is a smaller amount today and look forward to putting in more another day.

Preparing and Developing Your Goal Mindset and Beliefs Exercise

Write your goal here:

____

Check your goal is SMARTLY written and carry out any fine tuning until the goal is written SMARTLY.

Specific: you will be able to identify exactly what you aim to achieve. For example, double my income (insert amount) by (insert date).

Measurable: progress can be measured along the way as well as by the end date. For example, double income means each quarter you need to have increased your income by at least 25 per cent or a quarter (enter amount and date).

Achievable: I will be able to appear confident and share my ideas with a group of colleagues at the (date) meeting. Or I will increase my circle of friends and social life. I will attend at least two social events a week. I will develop my social skills and confidence by...

Realistic: Instead of, I will be an Olympic runner in one year. I do not know how fast I can run or if I will qualify. I will train daily to be able to run as fast as I can by (date). Rather, I will start training to run as fast as I can and join a running club to participate in races and regular coaching.

Timebound: Success and completion is measured in terms of time. I will start training daily from today and train every day for one year.

Loving You: The goal supports your values, strengths and talents, your aspirations and desires. The goal is for you, not what you feel you should do but what you want for you. It makes you feel energised, challenged, excited.

Having a SMARTLY goal allows you to action plan your progress towards having what you want.

How do you plan to go about achieving your goal? What are the steps you will take?

Are there any other ways you can work towards your goal?

What else may be helpful?

What do you need to help you achieve your goal internally?

What do you need to achieve your goal externally?

What resources/needs are you missing internally?

What resources/needs are you missing externally?

Cast Study

Here's a conversation I recently had with a client who wanted to lose some weight. By the way, losing weight is a negative and when I explained this, she restated her goal in the positive: I want to be 10 stone by 20 May. I am ready to let go of XX pounds/kilos.

How do you want to feel while you work towards your goal?

Client: "Good about how I look and confident I am getting slimmer; I can do it."

What sort of thoughts would you have if you felt like that?

Client: "Wow, it's really happening! I'm doing really well and my body is already feeling good. I am really enjoying that already I'm feeling good. I feel so much more energetic and healthier."

What would you do if you were like that?

Client: "I'd be happy to wear my clothes now and feel comfortable and confident about how I looked."

How would you be?

Client: "I'd be very confident and determined and enjoy following my new way of eating as it makes me feel so good."

The client worked on feeling good about her body, now, with some body confidence exercises and built up some energy and feeling healthy anchors too. The client and her friend sorted out some affirmations for her.

Here are the client's goal affirmations which are designed to install the new beliefs to achieve her goal:

My body feels good and supports me.

I am growing stronger and healthier every day.

I love my body, I'm loving me.

I am making progress step-by-step, meal-by-meal.

I feel confident, the changes are perfect for me. I deserve this so much.

To make your affirmations do the work for you, repeat them over and over, whenever or wherever you are. You just make them your mind wallpaper.

Repeat them as much as possible in your head and/or out loud. After doing an Mb exercise is super powerful too. Your affirmations are working inwards to install the beliefs that will ease your goal into being. How many times have you given up on something because you did not believe you could do it?

3D Directed Daydream

Daydream what it is like having your goal, bringing it into your reality; the mind is very straightforward—what you give it, teach it, it believes. Affirmations also trigger your reticular activating system, which will attract the opportunities to grow your goal into reality. As you daydream your goal make sure you focus on imagining your feelings and beliefs, too, when you have your goal, asking yourself to imagine how you will feel, what you will believe. In this way you focus on your most important inner world.

Use the Belief Changer Affirmation(s) Exercise to Support Your Goal

Make this a regular activity in your journal when you have a goal you are working towards. This helps you identify the things you think you are not so good at or are currently not your strengths but are needed for your goal achievement. Read through how you thought about yourself. Notice the areas you would like to improve, feel happier about. Pick just one to work on.

Follow the steps in the next exercise to create your own belief changer affirmations.

The client I talked about earlier who wanted to lose weight needed to feel much more confident about her body. Her belief about her body was ugly, fat, overweight, too big, clumsy. With all these beliefs rocking around in her head and reminding her of how *she felt* her body looked, do you really think setting a goal to lose weight and feel good about herself was going to work? She agreed to work on her body confidence as much as her healthy diet, to enjoy her body now, consider her body as something to care for rather than blame, feel ashamed of, driving her to hide away.

I asked her to work through the following questions and write down her answers, even add pictures or doodles to add what that may look and feel like for her.

Important note: When you have a goal that includes giving something up or losing something, understand our minds are hardwired to struggle with loss. Look for ways to release the unwanted behaviour, let go of, free yourself from, rather than focusing on loss or losing. For example, "I am happy to let go of XX kilos/pounds" or "I now allow my body to be free of any excess kilos". Your body is beautiful and has its own beautiful shape which is unique to you; it is time to fall in love with, believe in you, not a social media image!

Belief Changer Affirmation(s) Exercise

I have written in italics *if weight loss was a goal* in an attempt to make sure you fully understand the exercise. Answer the questions based on the goal, wish, desire you want to work on. This exercise is appropriate for any goal, not just weight/body image issues.

1. List the thoughts you would have if you had your goal/wish/desire (*were more confident about how you looked*).
2. What would it feel like if you were more/had your wish or desire (*confident about your body*)?
3. How would you act if you were more confident, had your goal/wish/desire?
4. What would you do if you were confident (*about your looks*)?

5. What would be better in your life?
6. What would you be able to do if you had more confidence?
7. What could you stop doing?
8. What could you start doing?
9. How would that make you feel?
10. What sort of thoughts would you then have?
11. If you felt good about (*your body*), what would you then have?

You can add questions or skip questions remembering that by answering these questions you are helping to clarify your intention steps towards reaching your goal. This is the "how to" part of allowing your goal to come in. If you get really stuck ask a trusted person, someone who truly cares, to provide your answers or help you find your answers.

Journal Tip

Get into the habit of reading your answers to these questions daily, just before you add your daily entry or update. If there is anything you want to change or add to you can then add it in your daily entry or better still you can write it out again each day. You now have a clearer picture of what you are creating for you and what you are welcoming into your life, and you are regularly reminding yourself. Now you work on everything, the whole new you, moving the focus to internal change rather than purely external change. It's the brain diet to really make your world change to reach your wishes and desires.

Start Building the Affirmations to Manifest Your Power

Some important reminders!

Affirmations must:

- start with "I am" or "I have". Sometimes it feels more comfortable to start with "I am beginning to"; that's okay too.
- always be positive. They always say what you want as if you have it already. They never state what you don't want, a lack, or fear creating.
- be easy to remember, to the point, specific, happening *now*!

For example:

- I am confident about how I look at work = good example
- I am beginning to feel/act/be more confident about how I look = this works. It's growth.

Sometimes the leap from lack to being is too much for us—after all we're not stupid!

- I don't want to feel awkward about my look at work = negative. It won't work how you want it to work. Your mind will misread it as "I want to feel awkward about my look at work". The subconscious mind (where this needs to take root) does not hear/see negatives and you get the affirmation minus the negative being learnt, stored in the part of the mind that holds our deepest beliefs.

Negatives Diminish the Positive

The subconscious, where these beliefs about ourselves are deeply rooted, is very black and white and does not work in negatives. It will only pick up on the positive; the negative affirmation would be interpreted as "I want to feel negative about my look at work". Or maybe if it's weight loss you instruct yourself, "I mustn't eat chocolate" and immediately the subconscious hears "I must eat chocolate". That's why once you start restricting yourself you find you want it even more. Far better to instruct yourself to eat "healthy foods that enable my body to feel healthy, firm and strong" or whatever it is you want your body to feel. Focus on the gain not the loss.

Framing Your Affirmations for Weight Loss or Any Kind of Habit Loss

I always explain to clients who wish to change something, do something differently (maybe stop biting nails or giving poor presentations at meetings, or to stop struggling when given deadlines, having a fear of writing reports or having shyness at the school gate or situations meeting new people, whatever the barrier for you), focus on what you want to gain and what you want to do—not "need to do" but "want to do"—to bring about the change you want. Really explore, get familiar with what you are creating for you. Affirmations are always about you.

The Focus Is on You

You cannot change other people, only you. However, if you change how you are, how you act, show up, it follows that other people will notice and therefore respond to you in a different way to closely match how you are presenting yourself to them. It is much more than looks, it's the way we move, hold ourselves. Next time you are out, notice people's body language and see what it says to you. Decide for yourself what you want to silently signal to the world and use the body language that goes with your chosen goal.

Your affirmations need to be used to do two important things: strengthen your self-beliefs about yourself, about others and the wider world and that you deserve and can achieve whatever it is you desire. Using the goal(s) you wrote in the goal-setting exercise, create your affirmations to accelerate your success.

Focus on what you want to bring into your life. Remember this is about you and meeting your needs. It must be about building you: your self-esteem, confidence, feelings, skills, talents and strengths to meet your goal.

Affirmation Creation Exercise

This exercise will help you find the perfect affirmations to achieve what you want for you.

Write down (or record on your phone if you prefer to talk your responses) your:

- thoughts you have now about your goal/aspiration/desire. Do you really believe you can achieve your goal/desire?
- thoughts about what others, your wider world, think and believe about your goal/desire?
- feelings about yourself and what you feel others believe about you?

- Actions. What are you doing each day to achieve your goal/desire? How are you acting/behaving?
- thoughts about what is next and what is possible for you now?

This exercise helps you identify and understand your existing beliefs around your goals/desires. After recording your thoughts, write affirmations that make sure or change your beliefs to enable your achievement of your goals/desires. No more than five or six. Affirmations are there to support and grow your mindset into a "can do" mindset with the beliefs supporting your deservedness and belief in your achievement.

For example:

Goal:

I wish to live a stress-free life

Current thoughts revealed from this exercise:

I have always been stressed and nervous. All my family believe I am always stressed and take after my great-aunt who was a very sensitive, stressed person.

New Affirmations

- *I am creating and enjoying a calmer mindset.*
- *I am reducing my stress levels every day by doing my exercises.*
- *I am naturally a calm person.*
- *I use stress to easily calm myself.*
- *My family are proud of me, support me, love and accept me.*

No magic involved. Affirmations are the tool to do the work, change beliefs to accelerate your success and create your success mindset. The example I have given came from a client who has successfully learnt how to manage her stress and build her resilience. She also talked to her family about how to best support her, by reminding her that it takes more energy to be stressed than to do the work and be calm. Her progress was fast and her belief in her own abilities continues to grow with her feeling able to take on bigger challenges.

Emotional Contagion

I have worked with many clients who often report that someone else suffers from stress in their close family and it is usually an older member. Emotions are highly contagious; spend an hour with someone who is very stressed, and it is likely you will leave them feeling stressed too, even if it is through frustration.

They will often report it runs in their family, and their mother and/or father are very stressed. This is likely a learnt behaviour in their formative years and has equipped them with the belief that they too suffer from stress and anxiety; it almost becomes acceptable. Consequently their world shrinks in an effort to control the stress. For example, avoiding new opportunities and challenges as they have the belief they cannot, or will not, cope.

Perfect Goals and Perfect Lives

Okay, you are now getting closer to what you want for yourself, and this is great. However, this presumes that you don't have a life right now, you don't have obligations or needs right now, only your goal exists and you're working towards it. This is where you need to make sure you create space and start to choose what needs to go.

Grow from a Place of Space

Guess what? No, you cannot have it all, but you can have all of what you need. Your life is yours! Regardless of your current obligations and commitments you need to audit them now, including your roles and responsibilities and choose them again, bearing in mind you are making space for your goals, your well-being and resilience growth.

Write down all of your responsibilities and all of your roles and approximately the time they take up. I have started the first one for you, which is a really important one for us all and it is *you*. How much sleep, rest and exercise do you need to function? Looking after yourself, your well-being and managing stress levels—using only "motivational stress" (which is regularly discharged) is essential.

Motivational Stress

This is the very short-term stress we use to help us focus and get on with whatever we need to do. It is short term and once we are doing whatever we need to do, e.g. run for the bus, stand up and do that presentation, we release the stress and focus, concentrate on what we need to do, and experience calm, not stress. When the event is over, we feel totally relaxed and calm, not fearful or edgy or whatever stress feels like for you.

This is you being you and loving life because stress and exhaustion is no longer your status quo but health, refreshing resilience and balance is now your status quo, no matter your aspirations. Your nows are opportunities not only to create your life and work towards your goals, they also are critical to running your engine smoothly, minding your gap between stress and well-being.

Creating the Space, Living in the Now

By repeating your affirmations you are gently training your mind to support you towards your goal. You do not need to stop anything; you only have to start to focus on what you want and need. Any time you feel uncomfortable use it as a trigger to focus on what you have decided you want. You are training your mind to work in a different way, in the now, dealing with exactly what is going on now, in this moment, in front of you and using that space to create your next moment. By checking and developing what suits you most, this enables your desires, and progress, to be uniquely yours. Through constant repetition, this way of directing your mind to suit you will become an automatic habit, deeply placed in the subconscious, the autopilot, replacing the stress habit with resilience, confidence and high self-esteem.

Whenever I realise that I am worrying or letting fear-based thinking creep in, I now take action and just refresh my mind with what I want. Now my trigger to look after myself is when I notice my mood drop or my stress levels growing too high. At most it takes me a couple of days to notice, and I realise I need to consciously do the keeper habits and very quickly my resilience, confidence and self-belief are supporting me. Clients report the same; how quickly the keeper habits help them in challenging times once they have installed all three keeper habits. The more you place yourself in the now, the stronger you are, and you have the space to select what boosters you may need and quickly feel the benefits. You are living through your confidence and strong self-esteem.

It's Natural. Just like Bacteria, Some Are Good for Us and Some Not!

I believe we all have wobbles when our confidence decides to hear, see or feel what I call the confidence smasher, real or imagined. For example, I can and do get lots of great feedback from my clients on how well they are doing and thank me for their help but just one negative comment rings in my ears for several days after. I want to be able to do my best for the clients that work with me but rather than use feedback as information to inform my work, negative bias can take over.

Negative bias is a healthy human trait designed to keep us safe, not stuck or stressed! Running too high, that natural safety mechanism glues us to the spot creating an unreal now, signalling too much stress. If we are not regularly discharging our stress the negative bias runs too high, and stress becomes our now. Using Keeper Habit One and staying in the now, discharges stress and allows us to access our natural confidence, our self-belief, as a norm.

Belief and Your Goals

So far you have worked on making sure your beliefs match and support any goals and aspirations you hold to accelerate your success. The next chapter helps you to work on any beliefs that may be holding you back but are not necessarily linked (according to you) to your goals and aspirations.

Our Belief Systems

Beliefs are often so deeply buried we are not aware of them but silently they run our lives, shape all our decisions, choose the company we keep, and form our interests, likes and dislikes, successes and failures. These belief structures are resolutely accepted by us, they are like our inner "running machinery" and dictate the quality of our life, our aspirations and expectations now and in the future.

Change, Including Belief Changing, Is a Process, Not a Switch

Recognising change as a process rather than an instant fix helps us to be kinder with ourselves and more likely to achieve success. Accepting change as a process helps you to recognise you can change anything when you accept and follow the process of change. You can resist the urge to give up whenever things do not "change" as quickly as you desire and use the information acquired to plan how to create the change you desire to more closely match your needs.

Allow the Inner Critic to Come and Go

Any change is made up of many steps and when you are in the process of a change rather than berating yourself if you slip up, simply go back to the planning stage. Accept that "slip ups" and "relapses" are a part of the change process and provide critical information for you to succeed further along the process each time. Be mindful. You are taking yourself into new territory and it can be scary. Why else would you have chosen those previous behaviours? Likely it was an attempt to keep yourself safe, driven by outdated beliefs inherited from some other place, person, experience or time.

Forget Switch, Go with Process

Our behaviours are frequently designed by us as an attempt to keep us safe. These behaviours, which are often deeply buried in our subconscious, offer some sort of payback, something necessary for us, likely based on a belief learnt long ago. This is often the case from behaviour habits to thinking habits to feeling habits, regardless of what our logical brain knows, expects or understands now. During the change process you are gently retraining your thoughts and emotions to bring about the actions desired; new thoughts and new feelings are being created to support the newly desired actions. Accepting this change helps you to help yourself through change and applaud your successful steps. Allowing the detours, delays or seemingly slow progress to be part of the change process is an indicator that you are changing and is an opportunity to learn, grow and replan your progress towards a completed change process.

Modifications Always Welcome, Learn to Flex

When we act with intention, we allow life to give us the unexpected bonuses; more than just a goal reached, we assist our inner world to grow, give ourselves time to learn, align and install the new beliefs to match the desired change. The map is not the territory; the goal is the destination, not the journey.

Exercise: Mapping Your Change Process

Map the change process you went through to install Keeper Habit One using the chart below with the example provided from one of my clients.

Example

Change Changes You, Your Inner Landscape, Your World

Approaching change as a process enables you to learn more about you and what is best for you, now, at this time. Imagine you have decided to follow healthy eating habits, and you start the day with a healthy well-balanced diet, take a nutritious lunch with you and then find during mid-afternoon you are so hungry you are tempted by the chocolate bars in the snack machine. You buy a small chocolate bar. You respond by allowing your inner critic to tell you what you should or should not have done, then have a choice—go back to your old eating habits, stay the same, or use this new information about yourself and go back to the "what's this telling me?" or "finding out stage" of the change process. Find out how you can balance your food intake so you can have something mid-afternoon and avoid the hunger pangs that made it too difficult for you to stick to the new eating plan.

Reflect on Your Change Journey
Introducing Keeper Habit One

Activity: Meeting Your Older Self (Hypnosis)

Find a place where it is safe for you to switch off from the world and you will not be disturbed. Sit or lie down in a relaxed position with legs and arms uncrossed, back and head supported and spine soft but straight. Close your eyes and take a deep breath.

Either listen to the recording at the link below or follow the script, whichever suits you.

Part One: Relax Mind and Body

- Take three slow deep breaths in... and release them slowly.
- With each breath out, imagine you are releasing any stress and tension in your body and mind.
- Now allow your breathing to settle to normal.
- Imagine a warm, golden light surrounding you, starting at the top of your head and slowly flowing down your body. This softens and relaxes your body and brings deeper calm and relaxation as it moves through you.
- Feel your arms, legs and shoulders becoming more deeply relaxed... softer... more at ease.

As you relax, notice that with each breath, your mind relaxes and softens. Any thoughts you notice gently float away like clouds in the sky. You are safe, you are calm, and with every breath feeling calmer still.

Part Two: Relax Deeper

Imagine yourself standing at the top of a beautiful staircase. If there is anything you do not like, you find you can change it just with a thought.

The staircase has 10 wide steps and leads you gently downward, has a firm handrail and at the bottom is a peaceful space where you feel safe and secure.

> With each step down, you relax even more. Count the steps as you go down and feel yourself relaxing deeper and deeper, all is calm, all is peaceful.
>
> 10... stepping down...
>
> 9... deeper and more relaxed...
>
> 8... calm and peaceful...
>
> 7... letting go of all remaining tension...
>
> 6... halfway there, feeling so relaxed...
>
> 5... so relaxed, so calm...
>
> 4... deeper now...
>
> 3... almost there...
>
> 2... feeling completely at ease...
>
> 1... deeply relaxed and ready to meet your older self.

Part Three: Imagine

- Imagine yourself standing in a beautiful, peaceful space. It could be a garden, a peaceful woodland, or a beautiful beach—whatever feels right for you is perfect.
- In this space, there's a pathway that leads you to a special meeting place. Begin walking along the path, enjoying being in this wonderful place, where you feel safe and secure and totally at ease.
- As you walk, you notice someone in the distance waiting for you. As you get closer, you realise this is an older version of yourself—someone who has lived a full and meaningful life.

Part Four: Spending Time with Your Older Self

- As you approach your older self, they smile and welcome you. You are so pleased to see each other. You both take a moment to look at each other. Notice how they look, how they carry themselves, and the peaceful energy they radiate.
- They invite you to sit with them and when you're ready, you begin a conversation.
- You could ask:

  What is the most important thing I should focus on right now?

What challenges have you overcome, and how did you do it?

What advice do you have for me at this point in my life?

- Allow the answers to come naturally. They may appear as words, images, or simply feelings. Trust whatever comes to you.

Part Five: Allowing

- When you are ready to leave and your conversation feels complete, thank your older self for their guidance and wisdom. Know that you can return to this place whenever you need their support.
- As your older self steps away, feel a sense of gratitude, self-belief and confidence growing within you.

Part Six: Returning to Now

- When you are ready, begin to bring your awareness back to your present self.
- Imagine the staircase again, and with each step up, feel yourself returning to the now, your present.

1... slowly becoming aware...

2... feeling refreshed and calm...

3… bringing back all the wisdom you've received…

4… feeling more awake…

5… opening your eyes, fully present and energised.

Stretch and give yourself a few moments to become fully awake, as if you have had a nap. When you are fully awake, gently carry on with your day. If you are doing this exercise at bedtime just allow yourself to drift off to sleep.

Reflection

Take a few moments to reflect on your experience. Either in the morning or after you have returned to your day, fully alert. You may wish to journal any insights or messages your older self shared with you, now, this evening and over the next few days.

Key Takeaways

How to use Keeper Habits One, Two and Three to increase your self-awareness, build your resilience and thrive:

- Generate internal and external goals for daily, achievable intentions that mirror your values.

- Check your goals and intentions are focused in your areas of control and influence.
- Use your journal to record your goal SMARTLY as a clear direction.
- Build your affirmations using exercises such as 3D Directed Daydreaming and Belief Change Affirmations to support your beliefs about your goals.
- It is essential your beliefs are designed and created to enable your goals.
- Build your self-belief and learn to use your inner wisdom to guide and support you.
- Approach change as a process that is much more than just a decision, and reflect on your change journey using Keeper Habit One.

Further Reading

Remember you have all the exercises you need on the podcast https://fionachapmanspodcast.buzzsprout.com/ and in your journal if you are journalling, which I highly recommend.

Working with Emotional Intelligence by Daniel Goleman

Coaching for Performance, 5th Edition by Sir John Whitmore

Cognitive Behavioural Coaching Techniques for Dummies by Helen Whitten

NLP at Work: Neuro Linguistic Programming, Third Edition by Sue Knight

CHAPTER 6

The Growth Mindset: Manifest Success, Keep Evolving

Harness the power of continuous growth and develop the mindset that attracts success in all areas of your life.

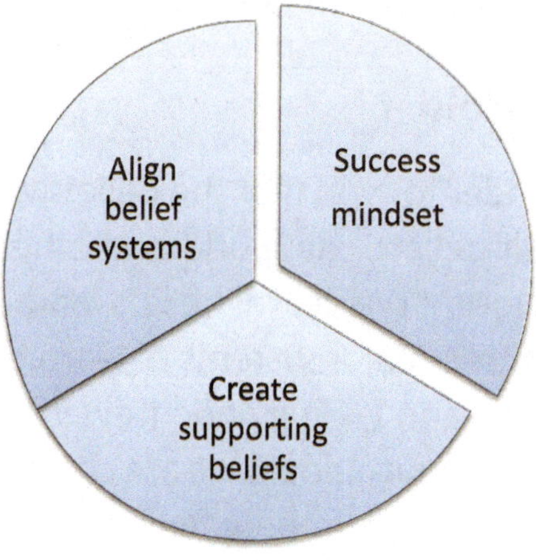

Building Your Success Mindset

So far you have chosen your goals and aspirations and devised some affirmations to boost your self-belief and focus on attracting, manifesting and achieving your goal. You can keep on growing your success mindset, opening your awareness to the real potential for you, your aspirations and run your life on success and positive self-belief. Self-belief is a part of your belief system and now is the time to align your whole belief system to maximise your success.

Beliefs to Accelerate Change

Making sure you hold the beliefs to match any change, in your internal and external worlds, is how successful change happens. As your beliefs change to more closely match your aspirations so do your choices, preferences and the opportunities you notice to create and pursue your successful life.

Beliefs We Hold

This is a reminder for you that the beliefs we hold about ourselves (self-belief), the world and other people will shape our world. We learn beliefs and install them through the three major systems of learning: shock and awe, repetition, and feeling good (reward). As we grow as children and young people we are constantly learning through those significant people in our life: our carers, peers, teachers and those we deem to be an authority, or in authority. We do not, or very rarely, question the validity of the beliefs we adopt as we are reliant on these people in our lives for our survival and ability to cope. Sometimes beliefs can be installed through "trauma"; anything that feels traumatic for us will form our beliefs in one, two or all of the following areas: our beliefs about ourselves, the world and other people.

Wrong Spectacles

As beliefs form our view and understanding of the world, it is important that the beliefs we hold match who we are now and aspire to be. Beliefs form the engine for us to create the life we desire, the life we are capable of creating for ourselves. Beliefs are more than just thoughts, they are deeply held convictions that shape our thoughts, feelings, emotions, actions and ultimately how we engage with the world, with others, and shape our expectations and goals. Given that we learn our beliefs, as we grow and mature, from others, not ourselves, it is important to check the beliefs we hold are enabling rather than disabling our desires, goals, expectations, talents and strengths.

Aligning Your Beliefs

You have already begun to strengthen and grow your self-belief to allow you to live successfully by using

Keeper Habits One, Two and Three. Alignment is crucial to setting your compass, and aligning your internal and external beliefs to support your aspirations, goals and desires. When both parts of belief are in sync, we create our power to propel us forward to the life we desire and goals we wish to create. We believe we can do it deep down; we believe we deserve whatever we desire and have the capabilities to provide or access the resources to achieve whatever we want. Our life becomes our own, not a life created on beliefs learnt from others, for another time and someone else's life.

Case Study: Powerful Stuff

I worked in an education unit for troubled young people and one of those young people was a particular challenge. However, they were very bright and able intellectually, so the teaching was more about helping her gain the skills to learn, study and present her ideas coherently. It was obvious that the youngster believed college was a waste of time and the sooner she could leave, the better. This was at the early stage of my understanding of beliefs, so I asked her if she would be part of a project for my studies and she agreed. We worked on her beliefs about her abilities and her self-belief; she enjoyed the challenge. Fast forward two years later and someone shouted at me down the college corridor. It was this student, and she had just heard she had been accepted to university. She told me she would be the first ever in her family to go to university. The project she worked on with me had been about developing her self-belief and belief in her ability to succeed in study. If at the beginning I had asked her to set a goal, her goal would never have been to go to university, it would have been to leave college as her belief in education and her ability to learn were taking her in another direction. Beliefs most likely learnt from others and her experience, so far, of education. First, she needed to develop her self-belief and then explore the range of wider beliefs that could be available to her.

When It Goes Adrift

When our internal and external beliefs are misaligned to any goal or desire we hold, we consistently experience roadblocks and obstacles that ensure we do not succeed. For example, imagine you set a goal to earn double your current income in a year. If our self-belief and internal beliefs are predominantly concerned with self-doubt and a "never enough" mindset, achieving any financial goal is going to be fraught with struggle. Even if we do achieve the goal, it is likely we will lose the increased income as quickly as possible. Our inner conflict will strengthen the inner critic's cause and can even lead to feelings of imposter syndrome, where success is believed to be undeserved, not real and potentially triggering unconscious efforts to sabotage any achievement.

Using Your Self-Awareness

Using the keeper habits lowers the stress and allows your self-awareness to grow, notice what is happening for you and choose something different. Frequently, clients declare, "I know I shouldn't, but I cannot help it!" Now, you can help yourself. As you habitually lower your stress and direct your mind you create space, space to choose. As you choose the thoughts, feelings and actions to build you up, your resilience grows. The space created by the lower stress levels can now be used to strengthen you and align your beliefs to accelerate your success beliefs, your success mindset. This is helping you to the success you deserve. Now you understand how possible success is for you, why wouldn't you choose success, I wonder?

Manifestation, Not Magic

Manifesting our desires, our goals and our aspirations is not just the actions we take but the beliefs we hold which truly accelerate our progress and motivate us forward. Obstacles and setbacks are no longer terminal to our dreams and desires but opportunities to explore and experiment; to create what we desire, being confident we deserve the life we aspire to and have the capabilities to create the life we desire.

Dips in Motivation, Increase in Stress Levels

Understanding stress and lack of motivation are frequently a belief misalignment that can help us to help ourselves by doing the simple work to explore and align beliefs to propel ourselves forward. The following exercises help you to do the belief work with ease. Remember that any reluctance to do the following exercises is most probably an outdated, limiting belief that deserves attention and realignment now. No magic, just an opportunity for success!

The practical tools to align your inner world for success:

1. **Check out your values**: which ones resonate with your aspirations? Use them as a tool to set your external goals. (Use the results of the Must Have Pyramid, finding your values exercise in Chapter 4.)
2. **Design beliefs to support your success and achievement:** write out your aspirations and goals, and explore the beliefs you hold about them and importantly, design the beliefs that

will support your progress towards your goal and aspirations. (Use the Identifying Limiting Beliefs exercise to shape your beliefs to support your success and to enable you to successfully take each step and reach your goal.) Work on growing the beliefs that support you having, enjoying and realising your goal as much as the practical steps to reach your goal.

3. **Visualise success:** daydream living with your goal achieved, your aspirational life. Daydreaming is a powerful form of self-hypnosis, getting you used to living your success and aspirations. Explore the Daydream exercise (https://soundcloud.com/user-135417655/directed-daydreaming?si=f9b9eff934d347229fe3e779b24ed0d0&utm_source=clipboard&utm_medium=text&utm_campaign=social_sharing)

4. **Reinforce yourself:** search out environments, relationships, individuals, online groups, and so on, that hold similar values, aspirations and hopes as you. Positive external influences will reinforce and strengthen your belief systems and accelerate your success.

   And the final exercise to make it happen for you.

5. **Identify limiting beliefs:** the replacing beliefs exercises help identify the beliefs held by you

that need replacing and letting go of, to allow the new hopes to come into your life. Limiting beliefs are anything that you believe is in conflict with your desires, goals and aspirations.

Exercise: Identifying Limiting Beliefs Part 1

Self-reflection: use one of your regular Keeper Habit One exercises to clear your mind. Then write out these three headings, leaving enough space for your thoughts and current feelings/ emotions on each of these areas. This is not a grammar or spelling exercise, just let your thoughts flow.

- **My goals**/wants/aspirations
- **My self-belief**—self-esteem and confidence
- **My abilities**/strengths/talents which will assist me
- **My beliefs about me** achieving, having, living my goal/aspiration (if you have several, deal with each one separately).

Just allow your thoughts to flow and write them down; this is for you, no one else. If you get stuck, use a Keeper Habit One exercise and carry on or take a break and come back to the exercise later. Maybe you only have one or two thoughts against each heading—that is fine. The more you do this exercise, the more this process of self-reflection will become more natural to you.

- **Recognise patterns**: read through what you have written and ask yourself "Does this help me proceed to success or hinder?" Identify recurring thought patterns. Are they negative or positive, such as "I am not good at…", "I am not good enough or qualified enough" and so on. Identify those thoughts which limit you.
- **Explore past experiences**: reflect on past experiences which may have begun the shaping of these limiting beliefs. Do you recognise someone else's voice/sayings in there? Consider how early, previous experiences, influences, criticism and/or failures might have shaped your current mindset. Do this without getting into judgements and the rights or wrongs. You are looking for things to let go of and replace with what suits you now. The past is over, gone; you are finally parking it in the past, not reliving the emotions, pain or hurt but keeping the good things and filling

the gaps to support yourself. Only you can choose to support yourself and accept and discern the right support for you from other sources.

- **Get feedback**: discuss your findings, good, supportive and not supportive, and any struggles to succeed you have experienced with trusted others in your life, maybe family or friends. Listen objectively as they too will have their beliefs, and focus on listening, understanding what they are saying to you. Hearing out loud from others your limiting beliefs and then listening to their perspective on your beliefs can help depersonalise things and develop enabling beliefs. Even if you feel their perspective is not for you, do not judge it, use it to discern what suits you best. Just make sure you choose those others who really do support you; be aware of seeking approval from others as this may be a limiting belief in action. You are not seeking approval, you are just sounding out your inner world to check how it helps you. If you do not feel able to work with others in this way you may find time with a therapist/coach or trainer may help, or joining one of my courses to find a supportive tribe on your journey.

Feedback then moves you into Part 2 of this exercise.

Exercise: Transforming Limiting Beliefs into Empowering Beliefs Part 2

1. **Challenge negative thoughts**: actively challenge and question those negative and/or unsupportive beliefs. List the evidence to support those unhelpful/negative views and then list the evidence to disprove the negative belief. Ask yourself what you would think or believe if the reverse was true; the negative thought was just an assumption and perception. Write out a new belief that supports your success and consider adding it to your daily affirmations.

   For example, instead of "very few people earn a living from this area", choose "I can gain rewards in this area. People do earn in this area." Or you could create something new. My favourite is, "Follow your heart and the right support will follow."

2. **Challenge the source**: when a limiting belief comes from past experiences and/or past influences it is not an opportunity to get stuck in justifying why you are struggling or looking for someone to blame. It is an

opportunity to look at your life now, who you are now, and question the value of this belief for you and the life you are living now and wish to create. Does this belief hold any truth for you now, your aspirations and goals? Either the belief belongs to the past and needs parking, or it belonged to someone else, for someone else's life, not yours. When a limiting belief has been learnt from someone else, recognise they only had this belief and all its limitations to share with you. Question why it should be true for you; you are unique, different, living in a different time, so allow yourself to create a unique belief for your life—their belief was their experience, their limitation, not yours.

3. **Build empowering affirmations**: create affirmations that counter the limiting belief and transform the belief into a positive statement. For example, if you believe you are not clever enough, experienced enough, good enough, or whatever it is you believe, replace it with "I am capable and deserve to create the life I desire" or maybe "I am good enough, I deserve..." or "There is always something new to learn and experience, to gain as I do/start/begin... it is part of the journey. I can easily..."

4. **Daydream your success**: allow yourself to imagine yourself having, doing, being whatever it is you aspire towards and wish to manifest. Create a strong image in your mind of how you will look, feel, think, move and act. Get really familiar with this version of you and regularly, hourly, imagine this version of yourself and step into this version of you getting more and more familiar with it. Daydreaming is a powerful tool to change your mindset, create the winning mindset you desire and reprogram your subconscious for success.
5. **Set achievable goals**: break your goals down into small steps, daily intentions/ steps, and focus on each mini-step as a success. Living with intentions opens up your radar (reticular activating system) and helps you notice the opportunities and possibilities for success. Each daily step towards your goals helps you live with intention. Reflect each day on your success so far, on your daily success. Reflecting on daily achievements, however small, helps build the achieving, success mindset and accelerates the movement towards achieving your goals and aspirations.

Exercise: Creating Goal Accelerator Beliefs

Identify your goal/ aspiration	
Write down your specific goal. Make sure it is SMARTLY (see previous goal formulation exercise in Chapter 5 to create SMARTLY goals/aspirations, if you haven't got goals you are happy with yet).	
Identify your beliefs	
List all of your thoughts, beliefs and feelings about the goal. Include both positive, helpful to you, and unhelpful, negative, and all thoughts, emotions/ feelings in between. Do not be limited by the space here. Add another sheet if necessary for each part. Use the Beliefs Emerger exercise worksheet to really find out what is limiting you and what will propel you towards success.	

Challenge	
For each limiting, unhelpful belief ask yourself: What evidence supports this belief/ statement/feeling? Is this belief/feeling based on facts or assumptions? What would I say to a friend who held the same limiting belief/feeling?	
Create affirmations	
Craft affirmations based on your reframed beliefs about your goal/ aspiration. (Use the rules of affirmation building in Chapter 3.) Check your affirmations focus on the new, reframed beliefs and strengthen your self-belief.	

Exercise: 3D Directed Daydreaming (Hypnosis)

https://fionachapmanspodcast.buzzsprout.com/1882592/episodes/16355866-3d-directed-daydreaming

Take three deep even breaths and visualise yourself achieving, living and having your goal as part of your everyday life. Imagine how you will feel, emotionally and physically. Picture yourself being successful, having your goal/ aspiration, and imagine how you will feel. What will you be thinking? What will you be saying? Who, if anyone, will be with you? How will you walk, sit, behave, move having your goal? Really enjoy and amplify all the positive emotions, feelings and actions you will experience when you succeed. Enjoy it all now. (Regularly revisit your daydream as you go about your day, as you drift off to sleep. Make it a regular practice to support your success mindset taking root.)

Reframe Your Experience into Success

For each negative, unhelpful and limiting belief/feeling and thought, rewrite or rethink it into a positive, enabling statement, feeling and thought.

Write the Future into the Now

Write down or draw how your success is going to be for you. (The drawing can be anything and does not have to be like a picture. It can be your favourite colours and shapes, a doodle, anything that makes you smile or feel good.)

Take time to record every detail or create a picture that represents feeling good, strong, confident and successful for you. Imagine you already have the goal and finish the following sentences. Use the feelings/emotions/thoughts experienced in your self-hypnosis session (3D Directed Daydreaming exercise).

Manifesting the Goal

Explore as much as you can so you really understand what you want, the impact of the changes on you, your life and maybe those around you.

When I am... or, When I have... or, When...

1. I am/I have ____________________
2. I feel confident because now I ____________________
3. My day/ daily routine is like this ____________________
4. I am able to ____________________
5. I now look forward to ____________________
6. I (do/learn/ develop/grow) ____________________
7. I easily ____________________
8. I feel (describe those emotions in detail)

9. My days are

   I am

   My surroundings are ____________________

10. How does this affect those that are important to me? (If it matters to you what others will think, do, then ask them! Don't expect to know what others will think, do, feel!) ____________________

11. How do I know these things are right for me? ____________________

12. What do I now believe about myself? ____________________

13. What do I believe about others? ____________________

14. What do I believe about the world? ____________________

15. My beliefs about myself ____________________

You may not have all the answers, and some questions may seem repetitive to you, but by asking the question you will start the process of having your goal and begin to find the right answers for you.

Trusted Supporters and Support

Find someone who can support you, share your goals and what you will achieve, share your feelings and emotions, and share the steps you take daily towards your goals, intentions, successes and opportunities to find different ways to success. Keep it going.

Experience Tells Me

While working with clients and importantly, myself, over the years I have learnt the contents of this book are definitely a winning starting place if you are ready to put your energies into successful living rather than stressful living. However, as your increasing self-awareness begins to help you to help yourself there may be some things that are deeply ingrained and though you can solve those stressors each time they come up, if they keep reoccurring it may be that they need a bit more work to get to the root of the issue. Obviously, a therapist can help you with this or you can continue to do the work for yourself, when you know how.

Use the Rule of Three

The rule of three is a useful one to remember. I have already discussed that using three improvement thoughts to diminish the impact of one unhelpful thought is a beneficial approach to using affirmations and power booster thoughts. In a similar way, if you experience something that does not enhance your inner world for three or more times it is something you can work on and improve. If something keeps coming up for you, a barrier to your confidence, your well-being, then it is a signal that whatever is bothering you has deep roots. By this I mean threats to unbalance your inner world keep happening from external circumstances and just happen with different people, places and situations. For example, many of your friendships after a lengthy period end badly; you keep choosing partners, relationships, which end up making you feel insecure, not good enough, and so on. Rather than keep clearing it up by using the three keeper habits (which will work) the best thing to do is to clear what is behind this pattern of behaviour.

Case Study

A client I worked with came to me because she felt her life was a mess. She had just left a relationship where she felt her partner did not treat her well. And someone who she thought was a trusted friend had just treated her, she felt, very unfairly—especially as the friend knew how upset she was after her relationship breakdown.

Together we explored all her important relationships and how they served her. She realised that all her romantic relationships had ended by her being left, sometimes quite suddenly, and in her own words, she felt she has never been able to rely on anyone as they always let her down. This was a belief for her that she firmly believed was true and the evidence was apparent in her experience of being constantly let down.

I also asked what she did to make this belief true for her? Was the behaviour unique for her past partners, or even friends? When she explored the behaviour of people she chose as partners and friends, she realised that many of them had previously acted that way with others. This is an example of how powerful beliefs can be working for us. Making sure your beliefs are fully aligned with your desires and wants is critical to changing things and bringing new things into your life.

This client explored the possibility she was subconsciously selecting partners/friends who left or let people down. She was able to find many occasions when she had an awareness of partners/friends leaving or letting others down. She developed a new belief and worked on installing the new belief. She also made a list of what she wanted from a partner and a friend to fit her new belief alongside working on her self-awareness and self-belief in her deservedness and worthiness of the types of relationships she wanted to have in her life. Fast forward several years and she reported that she is now in a stable relationship with someone very different than previous partners but is feeling very secure and confident in her partner and future. She had also thinned out her friendship group, which was hard being single, but she had found people who she knows she can rely on.

Key Takeaways

How to build your success mindset:

- Check your internal and external beliefs are aligned to support your aspirations, goals and desires.
- Use the keeper habits to lower stress and allow self-awareness to grow.

- Work on reducing your limiting beliefs using the Identifying Limiting Beliefs and 3D Directed Daydreaming exercises.

Further Reading

The Art of Happiness: A Handbook for Living by HH Dalai Lama and Howard C Cutler

Positive Intelligence by Shirzad Chamine

Words That Change Minds: Mastering the Language of Influence, Second Edition by Shelle Rose Charvet

Form a group of supporters, join an online group/course, visit my website (www.fionachapman.online) to support you. Keep using the tools in this book to keep you strong and to keep you in the success lane rather than the stress lane of life.

Keep Growing: You Are Designed for Your Best Life

The three keeper habits are just that, keeper habits, available to you always and once installed, quickly become part of your daily mental diet to keep you fit and healthy. Just as physically we need to eat, exercise, drink fluids suitable for good health in our bodies you now have the knowledge to keep your mind healthy too, attending to your well-being in a way that suits you as you go about your everyday life.

As your awareness increases, and you start to really live your life according to your needs, you may come across occasional "roadblocks" to your continued success. I have put together a resilience toolkit just for you, *How to "Mind Your Gap" to Living Successfully and Not Stressfully*, full of more specific, extended tools that you can now use with your increased self-awareness and knowledge of how to work with your mind and secure your permanent successful living. This book's title is *How to "Mind Your Gap" to Living Successfully Not Stressfully, Book 2: Your Resilience Toolkit*.

Maybe you will never need to include Book 2 in your toolkit to a stress-free inner world and therefore outer world. To help you know when, and if, to search out Book 2 and to include more tools in your successful living toolkit, here is a handy checklist of the tools included in Book 2. However, you may recognise something that bothers you too much already and choose to work on now using your increased self-awareness to your stress-free advantage before any more damage or stress has to happen again.

1.	Body confidence	Enjoy and feel confident about your body now. Allow yourself to create the best version of your unique body while enjoying exactly how you are now. Enjoy nurturing and naturally supporting your body to be at its best.
2.	Being you at your most confident exactly when you need it	Need to be at your best for that important conversation, meeting, date, event, presentation? Set up a confidence trigger to help you to success.

3.	Change those negative thoughts to supporting, positive thoughts	Break the habit of constantly running yourself down, worrying and stressing about your future.
4.	Critical voice: dissolve its power every time it shows up	Critical voice is something many people experience but you can now remove its power with just a thought and trigger confidence too.
5.	Control and influence: worry and stress	The only thing you have power over is yourself, your inner world, and that is all you need.
6.	Develop a strong "social" network	The importance of relating to your "tribe" in real life.
7.	Decision making	When making decisions feels too much, too difficult, too onerous. When we find ourselves stuck and unable to make a decision.
8.	Energy leaks, emotional contagion	Mental geography allowing you to be you and keeping yourself separate.
9.	Experiment, forget fail	Adopt an experimental attitude to you, your life, and grow.
10.	Feelings as a guide, not fact	Your self-awareness is your power, not your brake.
11.	Forgive yourself and others	Forgiveness, how to create freedom from all those draining emotions of blame.

12.	Guilt and shame	Live the saying "the past is a place we can never revisit only learn from" and choose for our now and future nows.
13.	Gratitude	Use gratitude to boost your mood and release your appreciation of you and others.
14.	Identity check	Making sure your ego is not gobbling up your happiness.
15.	Judgements	Avoid getting caught in the judgement trap, use them to discern what you do want, like, enjoy, etc.
16.	Keep challenging yourself	There are no failures, only growth, information and opportunity.
17.	Letting go of past hurts, people and humiliations	Simply letting these things fade into our personal, past history and cutting the hurt, fear and stress out of your life.
18.	Look after yourself	Listen and respond to your body and mind.
19.	No mistakes, just experiments	Getting unstuck. What would you do if you could not fail?
20.	Money and creating abundance	Understand money and abundance is limitless when focusing on what we have now.

21.	More self-belief boosters	Motivation, self-esteem and/or confidence seem not to be flowing? Use the keeper habits to recover from any knockbacks quickly.
22.	Negative outlook	Feeling threatened constantly, unsafe, fearful? Learn to balance and tip your outlook in your favour.
23.	Procrastination	Avoiding or putting off tasks and actions, yet constantly being aware of the need to start, continue and finish.

Keep in Touch

Finally, my intention for this book is to share with as many people as possible how to live a successful life, and as you know by now that means a stress-free life for me and you. Imagine if you could only trigger stress as a good, helpful state, to help you perform at your best and then relax into your best performance rather than experience ever-growing, too-high stress that just tumbles you into anxiety and ill health. I believe it is possible once you know how to look after your powerful mind that is only trying to keep you safe, relaxed and happy if only it understood how to operate in this modern world. Now you have the knowledge to make it happen for you, successful living rather than stressful living. I look forward to hearing how you get on. Please share and keep in touch on my website where there is a contact button for you to let me know (www.fionachapman.online).

Be Part of the Big Change and Share the Knowledge with a Million

I aim to share this knowledge via the books and courses with 500,000 people and I ask you to then share with just one person. A million people will now have the knowledge how to live successfully not stressfully in modern life and know how to "Mind Your Gap" between stressful living to enjoy successful living, always. That million will then pass it on and the myth of stress being our only way to cope, to live, will be buried forever. Who wouldn't choose success over stress if they knew how?

My Thank Yous

For being brave and trying something new, being prepared to live successfully and bring the real you into the world. Thanks for buying the book, too, and sharing the knowledge when you can. You now have the knowledge, the essential habits, to choose stress or success; every good wish from me and enjoy. You deserve success!

Further Reading

Cognitive Behavior Therapy, Third Edition by Judith S Beck PhD

Brief Rational Emotive Behaviour Therapy: 2 (Wiley Series in Brief Therapy & Counselling) by Windy Dryden

Neuro-Linguistic Programming Made Easy: An Easy to Read Guide on the Foundations of NLP by Jon Adams

List of Exercises and Activities with Podcasts Links

Chapter 2

Mindfulness-based exercise: Even Breath to Restore Your Focus

https://fionachapmanspodcast.buzzsprout.com/1882592/9531133

Mindfulness-based exercise: Soothing Breath

https://fionachapmanspodcast.buzzsprout.com/1882592/9531186

Mindfulness-based exercise: Naming and Calming

https://fionachapmanspodcast.buzzsprout.com/1882592/9612514

Mindfulness-based exercise: Self-Compassion

https://fionachapmanspodcast.buzzsprout.com/1882592/9579466

Mindfulness-based exercise: Toes and Feet

https://fionachapmanspodcast.buzzsprout.com/1882592/9531223

Mindfulness-based exercise: Sounds

https://www.buzzsprout.com/1882592/episodes/9531212

Mindfulness-based exercise: Body Scanning

https://fionachapmanspodcast.buzzsprout.com/1882592/9531151

Mindfulness-based exercise: Fingertips and Hands

https://fionachapmanspodcast.buzzsprout.com/1882592/9531159

Chapter 3

Exercise: Quick Self-Esteem Checker

Exercise: Your Self-Esteem: Pulling It all Together

Exercise: Tugging Your Anchor

Chapter 4

Exercise: The Needs, Talents and Strength Finder Exercise

Exercise: Must Have Pyramid: Finding Your Values

Chapter 5

Exercise: Manifesting Your Goal

Exercise: Success and Achievements Journal: Allow the Truth Out

Exercise: Preparing and Developing Your Goal Mindset and Beliefs

Exercise: Belief Creator Affirmation(s)

Exercise: Affirmation Creation

Exercise: Mapping Your Change Process

Chapter 6

Exercise: Identifying Limiting Beliefs: Part 1

Exercise: Transforming Limiting Beliefs into Empowering Beliefs: Part 2

Exercise: Creating Goal Accelerator Beliefs

Exercise: 3D Directed Daydreaming

https://soundcloud.com/user-135417655/directed-daydreaming?utm_source=clipboard&utm_medium=text&utm_campaign=social_sharing

About the Author

Fiona Chapman MA, DipAdEd, Post Grad Cert Clinical Hypnosis, NLP Master and Trainer, Diploma in Cognitive Behavioural Therapy, Diploma in Positive Psychology, Psychotherapy Diploma, qualified with "Coach Accelerator" Enhanced level Master Coach, Mindfulness Teacher and Practitioner Diploma, Master Trainer Reiki, certificate in EMDR and Ego State Therapy.

Fiona has spent many years working with young people and adults in education and professional development, leadership and management and for the past 15 years working as a therapist one to one and in groups to help clients live successful stress-free lives. Currently her two big goals are to help a million people live stress-free lives using the knowledge, she thinks, we should be taught before the three Rs or at least with them. Her other passion is creating a healing garden at her home in Dorset, if Hunter, the golden retriever, will stop eating everything!

Fiona says, "I am a great believer in 'practise what you preach' and in my thirties I realised I needed more from life rather than acting as if I was okay, coping but underneath just wondering how much longer I could get by. As I have explained in my previous book *The ChapWell Method: The 7 Keys to Your Success, Happiness and Wellbeing,* I tried many ways to support myself. Then, through study and my work, I started to develop my unique approach: a mixture of NLP (neuro-linguistic programming), CBT (cognitive behaviour therapy), hypnotherapy, psychotherapeutic approaches and mindfulness. From all of this I found a way for me to do modern life, working with my mind and our natural capacity to be the best we can be, no matter what. Never perfect, just human and loving life. My approach was so successful for me I began to share this way of doing modern life with clients, one to one, in groups, through writing and online courses and like me many others have found freedom from stress and anxiety."

Printed in Dunstable, United Kingdom

68099078R00141